*Theories of Inclusive Education*

# Theories of Inclusive Education
## *A Students' Guide*

Peter Clough and Jenny Corbett

P·C·P
Paul Chapman
Publishing

Paul Chapman Publishing
A SAGE Publications Company
1 Oliver's Yard, 55 City Road
London EC1Y 1SP

SAGE Publications Inc
2455 Teller Road
Thousand Oaks, California 91320

SAGE Publications India Pvt Ltd
B1/I 1 Mohan Cooperative Industrial Area
Mathura Road, New Delhi 110 044
India

SAGE Publications Asia-Pacific Pte Ltd
33 Pekin Street #02-01
Far East Square
Singapore 048763

**British Library Cataloguing in Publication data**
A catalogue record for this book is available from the British Library

ISBN: 978-0-7619-6940-2 (hbk)
ISBN: 978-0-7619-6941-9 (pbk)

Typeset by Anneset Typesetters, Weston-super-Mare, Somerset
Printed and bound in Great Britain by
Athenæum Press Ltd., Gateshead, Tyne & Wear

# Contents

# Acknowledgements

This book is based largely on data created within the Routes to Inclusion: Trends in the Development of Inclusive Ideology project. The project was carried out by Peter Clough and Jenny Corbett, and funded by our respective institutions; we should like to acknowledge the support given by the University of Sheffield Inclusive Education Research Centre and the University of London Institute of Education. At the centre of the project is a set of views and reflections shared with us by some 23 of our colleagues in the field; there would have been no project and no book without their – often brave – willingness to share with us the shape and scope of their careers within special and inclusive education. We are just as grateful to the teachers who allowed their coursework to be used as rich illustration of critical enquiry. Most of the interviews were transcribed by Tracey Earnshaw, and technical support was provided by Don Howes, both of the University of Sheffield. Our editor at Sage Publications, Marianne Lagrange, provided warm and critical support over the considerable period of bringing the book to its present shape – though any weaknesses are of course ours.

*Peter Clough* and *Jenny Corbett*
Sheffield          London

March 2000

# Preface: orientation

## How to use this book

We want this book to speak to you directly so that you can feel confident to debate the ideas it offers. Understanding the origins, trends and issues of inclusive education can be a difficult and daunting task, and theories on inclusive education can seem confusing and complex, often because the language used disguises the ideas. More than anything, we want as far as we can to use plain, simple language to convey complex ideas.

We decided to write this book because we were both becoming aware of how our own thinking had been influenced by different events, people, writing and ideas. We wondered in what ways this was true for other people working in the area of inclusive education and, particularly, how students working in the field could access the developing ideas of academics who have spent their lives carving out their own paths towards inclusion.

But do we *need* to know the basis of people's thinking? What use is it to understand something of the background of academics whose publications we draw upon in our present work? Should such texts just speak for themselves, and for the moment of their publication?

The view we are keen to urge in this book is that we are all part of a historical process. Whatever texts are, they are made by people and for people. It is people who give them meaning. So, for this very reason, we have to recognize that any publication will reflect a particular time in the writer's life history (and the same must be said for this book). People go on to change their views, add and develop them, and even adopt quite new ideological models – from the use of their own unfolding experience.

Why should these historical perspectives concern you? We think it is important that you locate your own thinking in terms of the perspectives and words of others. In this way, you can start to make explicit the hunches and explanations which underlie what you *think* and what you *do* in terms of inclusive education. Your own ideas and reflections on your experiences are just as important as those whose work is widely published and well known. In revealing something of the life work of the authors behind their publications, we want to encourage you – in a sense – to enter into a dialogue with them.

## What is different about this book?

There are a number of things which make this book distinctive in character. First, is it written primarily for students of inclusive education, rather than the academics whose ideas and writings contribute to it. Our own work with teachers studying for initial, higher and research degrees has led us to create this book in the way that we have, in the hope that it will be useful in our own teaching.

Second, this is a practical book and a further feature of its difference is that we have tried to make it easy to use. By this we do not mean that it is a book of 'tips' – rather it is a book which aims to make theories, trends and issues accessible for, as Kurt Lewin might have said, 'there is nothing so practical as a good theory'.This book does not seek to *prescribe* models of good practice. Nor does it seek to evaluate writers' thinking. Rather, through its original use of life-historical approaches to key authors and their work, we seek to demonstrate the links between theories, trends and practices, and in so doing we hope students will draw their own conclusions, make their own evaluations and identify for themselves models of best practice.

## How this book began

*Theories of Inclusive Education* as you see it now, began from a conversation we had early in 1998 about the books which had influenced our own thinking. We reflected, too, on how our own ideas had changed over the years and during so many different policy developments. Our observations were that different theoretical and ideological perspectives appeared to dominate at different times. For example, a psychological model of learning difficulty (as we understood it) seemed to characterize the 1950s and 1960s, whereas a disability rights model reflects the spirit of the early twenty-first century. Of course, as you work through this book you will perhaps realize with us that no thinking can be so neatly summarized.

It seemed to us, as we began thinking about the project, that this process of historical enquiry was a potentially rich way of helping students to recognize 'stages' in the growth of inclusive education. Our notion was that such a tracing of routes would, simultaneously, encourage students of inclusive education to locate their own experiences and reflections in terms of the 'larger narrative' (which in this instance is provided by a number of academic authors). This book does three main things: first, it provides a summary of five key positions or trends; second, it presents brief glimpses into the careers of many who have influenced the development of inclusive education; and, finally, it draws on the work of students whose own writing is seen to be working equally towards understanding and developing inclusive education.

In deciding where to begin, we interviewed those authors who had influenced us – in one way or another – in our own early development. These were Klaus Wedell and Peter Mittler, widely acknowledged as among the 'founding-fathers' of special education in the UK. We asked them questions which required them to reflect on their own influences and achievements. These included:

- How did you first become involved in the area of Special Education?
- Which example of research has been most influential on your own thinking?
- How have your own life experiences influenced your thinking?
- What particular example of your own work are you most proud of – and why?

While these two figures were an obvious choice to us, we had to think carefully about how we would go on to select a sample of the range of perspectives on inclusive education. We chose to do this in two ways: where convenient we interviewed and then wrote what we have called 'Profiles' of some of our authors. Others we asked to write their own personal accounts, which we call 'Reflections'. These two approaches have produced – in Section 2 of the book – a rich mixture of voices and perspectives.

There are, of course, many other people we could have talked to, and what we have produced here is not to be seen as a *Who's Who?* of inclusive education. It is inevitably uneven in places, reflective as much of our own personal experiences and hunches than of any specific historical analysis.

In our original conversation we had noticed too, how the notion of inclusion had seemingly emerged in a historical sequence. This sequence appeared to us to have begun with a psychological model dominating debates on special education. Gradually other models became influential in their turn and generated debates, first, on integration and then, more recently, on the concept of inclusive education. Important for us was the realization that the current conditions of inclusion might be discussed in terms of five perspectives which we have called:

- the psycho-medical model
- the sociological response
- curricular approaches
- school improvement strategies
- disability studies critique.

The writers in Section 2 reflect something of each of these various perspectives and their accompanying ideologies. Some of the authors we interviewed have been influenced (as have we) by several models, and few would see themselves as representative of only one model – even where a single perspective might have seemingly dominated a particular phase or stage of a person's work.

Finally, although a majority of the authors included here work in the UK, this book also draws on the work of some authors in North America and Australia. We are not suggesting that this illustrative sample is reflective of all those who are making significant contributions to the field. Our main concern has been to illustrate a range of perspectives and influences in order to demonstrate the complexity of inclusive education.

## The structure of the book

The book is organized into three sections. In Section 1, Peter Clough explores in more detail various theories, trends and issues within their historical eras, and their influence on inclusive ideology and practices. This first section provides a 'map' which broadly defines the territory to be explored. It illustrates the connectedness between one perspective and another.

In Section 2 we present an alphabetically ordered introduction to the sample of writers. We have written the Profiles ourselves, based on interview data. Each Profile gives a brief introduction to an author in terms of:

- 'sample' texts
- major influences
- quotations (from their sample texts)
- experiences of inclusive education
- relation to theoretical or other models.

The Reflections have no such format, but have been written by individual authors to express their own perspective – at this point in time – on their own career and contribution.

Section 3, the final section of the book, draws on examples of practice in inclusive education, where Jenny Corbett uses the writings of her students to show how their own work is knit with that of professional writers.

## The boundaries of this book

We hope that this book will be genuinely useful to you in working out your own position on 'the map'. Our objectives are that after reading this book you will be able to:

- express your own value position as an educator
- understand the range of various trends and perspectives
- show confidence in debate with the authors
- demonstrate how your own practice is informed by and relates to the various routes to inclusion.

We are aware of the limitations of our book. In concentrating on certain aspects of a sample of authors, the book does not offer a comprehensive critique of inclusive history, theory and practice. However, it is our intention in our work with students to use this book alongside other complementary texts, many of which are referred to and drawn upon throughout Section 1.

It can be argued that a particular limitation, in our discussion of inclusion is its specific focus on students with learning difficulties, sensory impairments or physical disabilities. In other words, we are concerned particularly with the historical relation of 'special' forms of education to emerging inclusive policy and practices. This is not because we see inclusion as narrowly occupied in this way: inclusion must be about the inclusion of all. But both of our own school-teaching and academic careers started in segregated institutions, and both reflect the shift and drift of policies from the exclusive to the inclusive. The story that we are particularly interested in, therefore, is the story of the emergence of inclusive ideology and practice within a situation – only 50 years ago – of statutory, categorical exclusion. So we are certainly not suggesting that the current inclusive thrust comes from special education; far from it. In fact, our interest is in quite the opposite process, in how *special education itself has been transformed from the outside* by civilizing forces which have deconstructed and reconstructed its meanings and effects.

Above all, this book is written as a tool for interaction and thinking. It invites – indeed depends upon – the reflection, critique, argument and discussion of its readers who will bring to it their own meanings, interpretations and understandings of the complex and ever-changing field of inclusive education.

# Section One

## *Routes to inclusion*

PETER CLOUGH

Tracing origins helps us to understand something of where we find ourselves today. I want to use this text to try out some ideas with you, the reader. It has been written as a tool for thinking. It offers some ideas and 'lenses' through which to view the recent history of inclusive education . . . and with which to argue!

# Introduction

## 'If only we had known then . . .'

*PC:* In 1978 I was working in a Special School, a school for kids with EBD . . . no, the point is that this was called a school for 'Maladjusted' kids. Can you imagine that now? I mean, this is only 20 years ago, and kids were called 'Educationally Sub-Normal' or – what? – 'Delicate', do you remember that. . . ?

*Paul:* . . . the categories . . .

*PC:* . . .11? 12?

*Felicity:* When I teach this now – Warnock and the '81 Act, the whole history of how we got to where we are today – it's difficult to convey how actually radical, how really radical it was at the time . . .

*Jane:* Did it feel radical to us then? I don't remember feeling it then, but looking back, looking back's much clearer.

(MEd seminar, Sheffield, September 1998)

### London, 1978

The government commission chaired by Baroness Mary Warnock reported to the government on the findings of its official enquiry into special education (DES, 1978). It was wrong, said the report, to identify children by means of their 'handicap', and then to send them to schools organized to deal with just such 'categories'. Rather, the report went on, we should identify their *educational* difficulties and provide accordingly. And so the term *special educational needs* (SEN) entered UK legislation, its classrooms and – importantly – teachers' thinking. Strange to think that it was only in the last 20 or so years of the twentieth century that we began to speak of special educational needs. Until then the official terms included such as 'maladjusted' and 'sub-normal'. Warnock's committee started to change things.

Perhaps as many as one-fifth of the school population – said the report – might have a *Learning Difficulty* at some point, and for some variable time, in their school careers. Some of these difficulties would be so distinct that the law would require an official *Statement* of the need they represented and – more importantly – a detailed prospectus of how these needs would be met. Thus a further term entered the jargon of educational difficulty and so the IEP – the *Individualized Education Plan* – became part of teachers' vocabulary. Many of Warnock's recommendations became law in the UK through the enactment of the Education Act 1981, and this legislation – together with Warnock's report – provide an essential hinge for this book.

### *Sheffield, 2000*

I choose the Warnock Report as my starting point in this overview of developments towards inclusion because it *was* evolutionary, but also has a peculiar contemporaneity for this book. For at the end of 1999, Mary Warnock announced: 'If only we had known then . . . The *statement* has been a disastrous mistake.' Reflecting on the effects of the committee's work, Warnock said:

> looking back on the days of the committee, when everyone felt that a new world was opening for disadvantaged children, the most strikingly absurd fact is that the committee was forbidden to count social deprivation as in any way contributing to educational needs . . . The very idea of such a separation now seems preposterous.
>
> (Warnock, 1999)

Of course, Warnock is herself a scholar – a philosopher at that – and might quite properly come to see earlier work as incomplete, or needing refinement. But, *disastrous*? *preposterous*? If Warnock is right in her assessment (admission even) – that the commission was wrong – then how ever should we justify the many thousands of experiences (of *statementing* and beyond) that characterize special education policy during the last 20 years?

That specific question is raised here to illustrate and emphasize two key points which are illustrated in this book: first, that

consensual ideas about who or what is 'special' change, sometimes rapidly; all such definitions belong to particular historical moments and are reflected in contemporary policies;

and, second, that:

individuals' ideas may change – sometimes radically – over the course of a career, and are in a dynamic relationship with policy contexts; this is to say that they may directly *influence*, as well as be *influenced by*, the development of policy.

## Constructing difference and difficulty

This was the first time in her short career that Steven's reception class teacher had had a child with a statement in her class. She was conscious that by choosing the inclusive option Steven's parents had accepted that he needed to interact with his peer group and not become, once more, dependent upon adults. She was reassured by the head that it was not a scenario of 'success or failure' and was given support to evaluate her own practice in a way which led her to believe that her established skills of providing a well structured and stimulating learning environment for all children were particularly relevant for Steven. She realised that it was her duty to attend not only to what was 'special' about Steven but also to what was 'ordinary' and that there was no mystique to analysing tasks. She was already doing this and making them accessible to all children, including children with learning difficulties.

(Herbert, 1998, p. 103)

Teachers, head teachers, parents make decisions about children and their difficulties, and behind every decision made in response to an instance of educational difficulty, there lie traditions of practice that more or less evidently affect outcomes. The decisions made by parents and teachers in the case discussed above by Herbert pointed to an outcome of *inclusive* practice. How an individual teacher, a department, a school, a local education authority (LEA) or service *constructs* both a problem and its solution is determined by their characteristic habits of interpretation. In the example above, Herbert draws attention to the transferable skills of a teacher of 5-year-olds to 'analyse skills' and present learning situations to children in ways which fit their own individual needs. It goes without saying that other interpretations may well be made, dependent upon experience and upon cultural determinants.

The sum of these various constructions of learning difficulty makes for a community with often diverse views on what 'special educational needs' are, and on how they should be met. Not all these views are made explicit as statements. They are more likely to be *inferred* from particular organizational structures: *this* LEA has closed nearly all its special schools, while *that* one is actually still building them; this school has a clear practice of withdrawal, while that one has subject-based learning-resource teams – of which the head teacher is a key member – and so on. But in each case these responses to educational difficulty express, if only implicitly, particular constructions of educational need.

This section of the book centres on the following questions:

- Where do the various 'constructions' of difficulty come from?
- How are they evidenced?
- How are they communicated?
- How are they challenged?
- How do they change?

> We are all in some ways involved in this process of influencing and being influenced by people and events, which is a process of making history. Academic study in this area ought to start from a point of discovering and articulating *our own place* within the weave of ideas that make up policy and its realization in people's lives.

Most important of all, within the context of this book, is the question:

*Who changes constructions of educational need, of difference and of difficulty?*

The brief biographies in Section 2 will provide some insights into the life experiences, theories and practices of those who work as academics in the field of special educational need and inclusive education. But before glimpsing those more personal perspectives we need to be clear about terminology.

### *Exploring perspectives on inclusion*

The term 'inclusive education' has itself come to mean many different things which can in itself create confusion for students in this area. It is in fact a contestable term used to different effect by politicians, bureaucrats and academics. 'Inclusion' is not a single *movement*; it is made up of many strong currents of belief, many different local struggles and a myriad forms of practice. As bold moral and political rhetoric – the stuff of banners – the urge to inclusion is easily expressed in Western countries.

However, the notion of an inclusive society is at the same time difficult to contest in moral terms. As a basic tenet of belief, should not everybody have the same rights of access to education? Of course. But after the bold print of the banners, when decisions have to be made about how more precisely to spend public monies, general ideas of inclusion become entangled and infected with specific individual interests. It is often at this stage that what was intended to be a uniform platform may disintegrate into more fragmented demands for 'positive' discrimination – that is, for *un*equal treatment in respect of this or that group. The argument for absolute inclusion has yet to be won, let alone realized in practice.

It is at this point that the *process* of generating inclusive educational practices reaches to the heart of policy-making. What is established as policy must be concordant with what actually happens in schools, and in the lives of pupils. In this respect Len Barton has argued a major role for inclusive practices in education in order to realize wider changes in society:

Inclusion is a process. Inclusive education is not merely about providing access into mainstream school for pupils who have previously been excluded. It is not about closing down an unacceptable system of segregated provision and dumping those pupils in an unchanged mainstream system. Existing school systems – in terms of physical factors, curriculum aspects, teaching expectations and styles, leadership roles – will have to change. This is because inclusive education is about the participation of all children and young people and the removal of all forms of exclusionary practice.

(Barton, 1998, p. 85)

This emphasis on inclusion as a process – rather than a specific ideology or set of practices – is reflected in the shape and character of this present book, in which is assembled a great range of perspectives. The concern here is not to make judgements as to which approach may be morally superior or preferable, but rather to show how different ways of seeing 'the broad picture' will influence the detail of practice and provision. Not only are interpretations of what inclusion means contentious, but there are also diverse and conflicting debates in which these different approaches are seen as detrimental to the effective development of this area.

## Theories of Inclusive Education: some key perspectives

The organization of this book as a whole is based on the identification of a number of writers whose texts have been – in different ways, and at different times – significant in the development of inclusive educational practices. I have chosen to look at these writers and their work in relation to five 'key perspectives', a loose framework for analysis developed from a reading of the 'Special', 'Integrative' and 'Inclusive' literature, and – importantly – from other influences which might hitherto have been regarded as 'mainstream' developments.

This framework of perspectives is like a map of territory partly charted and partly known only as we travel through it. The history of 50 years ago is obviously easier to write than the history which is being made in this moment. In constructing this map I have drawn on existing analyses – for example of the 'Individual' and 'Social' models of disability (Oliver, 1988) which are broadly recognisable. Analysis of more recent developments, however, is much more speculative and will, undoubtedly, be challenged and revised.

Of course this is not the *only* way to analyse the development of such ideas. Lipsky and Gartner (1997), for example, describe the 'evolution of ideas' in the USA in terms of three 'eras':

- the era of institutions
- the era of deinstitutionalization

- the era of community membership.

In their review of the US literature they consider a series of 'Focal questions' in relation to each of the 'eras' they have identified. Their book *Inclusion and School Reform: Transforming America's Classrooms* (Lipsky and Gartner, 1997) discusses many of the issues raised in our book here, but the framework for analysis is different, thus illuminating different cultural perspectives on the evolution of inclusive ideas.

For the purposes of our book, the review of literature leads to the identification of five major perspectives (Figure 1.1). These perspectives are never wholly exclusive of each other, nor are they strictly chronologically sequential. The construction of the model in this way is intended to demonstrate three things:

- the historical influences which shape current views and practices
- the heterogeneity of inclusive ideology
- the ways in which researchers' ideas change and develop over a lifetime.

The presentation of these five perspectives in the sequence shown in Figure 1.1 conveys a particular view of the historical development of ideas and of practice. Of course, in practice nothing is so neat; ideas and

---

**The psycho-medical legacy**
This is understood as the system of broadly medicalized ideas which essentially saw the *individual* as being somehow 'in deficit' and in turn assumed a need for a 'special' education for those individuals.

**The sociological response**
This position broadly represents the critique of the 'psycho-medical legacy', and draws attention to a *social construction* of special educational needs.

**Curricular approaches**
Such approaches emphasize the role of the *curriculum* in both meeting – and, for some writers, effectively *creating* – learning difficulties.

**School improvement strategies**
This movement emphasizes the importance of systemic organization in pursuit of truly *comprehensive* schooling.

**Disability studies critique**
These perspectives, often from 'outside' education, elaborate an overtly political response to the exclusionary effects of the psycho-medical model.

---

**Figure 1.1** Five key perspectives on educational inclusion

practices sometimes converge, and at other times practices remain as the legacy of earlier conceptions and positions. I do not want to suggest that these positions are mutually exclusive; indeed, although there is something distinct about each of them, you will see that each one 'maps on to' the others in certain respects.

So the suggestion of a simple, linear development from one position to the next is to oversimplify the case. Rather, I want to show how there is always a dynamic relationship between the various perspectives. It would therefore be more realistic to consider the five as occupying – at times – the same ground but with different (sometimes *competing*) emphases and popularity. We might represent this development with the conceptualization in Figure 1.2.

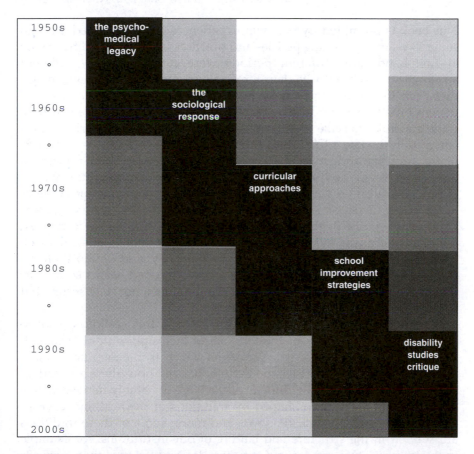

**Figure 1.2** A historical interpretation of the development and interaction of ideologies leading to present thinking in inclusive education

*Note*: It must be emphasized that the five key influences as I discuss them in this section are all ever present, but certain perspectives have their 'moment' and Figure 1.2 sketches the 'arrival' of those moments within each perspective.

## Routes and perspectives

*Ann C:* I think that those of us in special, in Special Schools that is, we saw 'Preventing Classroom Failure'- that objectives approach as a lifeline at the time ...
*PC:* Oh there's no doubt. Suddenly here was something with structure that you could actually ...
*Trevor B:* You could actually use positively. I mean, there just was no such thing as the curriculum as we'd understand it now, we were all just ... just doing our best, certainly, but flying without charts, I think.
*PC:* And the Ainscow stuff provided some of those charts? It did, it really did ...

(Teacher INSET course, Sheffield, November 1999)

This book is prompted by our own experiences. I have worked through some 30 years of changing policies and practices in schools, and have seen at first hand how different periods were conditioned by different approaches – each with its own terminology and ways of doing things; each with its 'gurus' and key texts. One of the first conversations with Jenny Corbett – similar to the one above – was about how we had both come gratefully to seize on some of the objectives-driven materials which emerged in the late 1970s. From the vantage point of 2000 – with its different priorities and policies – such behaviourist work seems quaint at best. However, in the 1970s curriculum guidance in any institutional form of Special Education was scarce, and such highly programmatic schemes as *Preventing Classroom Failure* (Ainscow and Tweddle, 1979) were a potentially rich resource in the curricular wasteland of Special Education. At this time, there was talk of how the school curriculum in general was a 'secret garden', to which only teachers held the key; and Phillip Williams commented that if indeed the ordinary curriculum had been a secret garden, then in Special Education that garden had been not only secret, 'but neglected, too' (Williams, 1985, p. vii).

In working some of the Routes to Inclusion in this section, I want to indicate the impossibility of thinking about inclusion without acknowledgement of the exclusive practices from which it is emerging. Raising the idea of a 'legacy' in this context emphasizes how there are certain ways of looking at learning difficulty which are inevitably handed down. Many of these have been shaped by traditions of medical and psychological practice going back 100 years and more. Some of these traditions are still felt in the structure and culture of our institutions, for example in the language that we use and the attitudes to difference that it reflects (Corbett, 1996). Other traditions emanate from a religious – if not biblical – view of difference and *de*/formity as ills to be cured. The 'legacy', therefore, of the medical model of disability is one which constructs disability as a problem to be solved or contained with procedures tried and tested much as medical remedies; a parallel structure exists in the 'psycho-medical' response to learning difficulties.

## *The psycho-medical legacy*

When we hear talk of the 'psychological' or 'medical' model, the terms suggest both a conformity of definition and an easily identifiable use and practice. But in reality there is no such orthodoxy in either term, and they have little meaning unless understood alongside the 'social' (or other) model which provides a critique of them.

It is important to understand, though, that while the terms may not have a distinct *conceptual* identity, their use does strongly imply an *operational* meaning. To talk of a 'medical' model in the context of learning difficulties is to point to practices which call on pathology (that is, a science of *disease*). Figure 1.3 points up some of the features of a medical practice.

It is a truism that 'special' education owes its origins – and, its critics would say, its shortcomings – to the development of a *pathology of difference*, first through medical, then, later, through psychological enquiry.

It is, after all, less than 40 years since clinic-based assessments were prevalent; typically, those involving school doctors, psychiatrists and, to a lesser extent, educational psychologists. Assessment was mostly carried out in one session, when normative testing – particularly full-scale intelligence tests – would be accompanied by 'projective' testing of personality. The chief purpose of this testing was simple: it was to determine whether the child required transfer to a special school of a particular category.

In the early 1970s there was a significant expansion in the training and deployment of psychologists, and a complementary shift of focus from clinic to school, where 'remedial' services practised degrees of 'withdrawal' from the classroom for additional help with basic skills. Educational psychologists started to rely less on 'global' scores of IQ, and rather on specific sub-tests of the Weschler Intelligence Scales, the Illinois

---

The 'medical model'

| *focuses on* | *rather than* |
|---|---|
| sickness | health |
| aetiology of the problem | experience of the individual |
| subject-specific pathology | environmental factors |
| specific treatment | holistic support |
| reactive measures | preventative measures (etc.) |

*Source:* adapted from Bailey, 1998, p. 49

**Figure 1.3** Some characteristics of the 'medical model'

Test of Psycholinguistic Abilities, or the Frostig Test of Visual Perception. As Williams (1990) points out, results of such batteries of testing were 'related to educational programmes designed to "strengthen" the cognitive or perceptual deficits assumed to underpin the particular subtests' (*ibid.*, p. 1026).

But this sort of assumption of a direct link between the 'training up' of individual deficit and consequent educational progress was not borne out in evidence as Ysseldyke (1987), among others, pointed out. For all this, such moves nevertheless represented an important shift in the development of educational assessment as importantly linked with intervention strategy. Some of Wedell's work, for example, during this period exemplifies a use of quasi-experimental hypothesis-testing leading to systematic intervention (Wedell, 1970).

But at the heart of these approaches was a view of the individual child as somehow deficient. Now although this deficit could be located and described by psychometric testing, its identification was made almost exclusively 'within' the child and not in the context of instruction. No connection is implied between the nature and presentation of a given task, on the one hand, and the child's performance of it, on the other. Today this seems an obvious shortcoming. But in the context of the 1960s (and to some extent 1970s) there was little or no apparent recognition of this in practice, for the curriculum was not as it is understood today. Nor were processes of learning articulated in the ways in which they have been in the later years of the twentieth century.

Before the term 'integration' was introduced formally in the 1978 Warnock Report and the subsequent legislation of 1981, some positive examples of integrative if not inclusive practices were developing. These could often be found within hospital settings and in the work of educational psychologists. Both Klaus Wedell and Peter Mittler, for example, might be seen to be exploring, in their separate and different ways, the routes to integration in their work of the late 1950s and early 1960s, long before the term 'special educational needs' was conceived.

In his work in Bristol, Wedell was encouraging hearing-impaired children from a segregated unit to join in mainstream classroom activities. Of this work, Wedell said (some 40 or so years later):

> I wasn't thinking of being inclusive. It was just that that was what I felt education was about then. One of the things I have always been concerned about is that *kids themselves should as far as possible be able to decide*. Later on we saw some videos of kids with severe physical disabilities who were integrated. Some of the kids that were integrated were marvellously sociable and the teachers were marvellous and the kids were marvellous but [the school] couldn't provide the physio[therapist]. If you saw the video . . . the kids were actually becoming less dependent but I also had to ask myself 'Who's being God, in making decisions for these kids? What is most important for them for the future?' They are going to be marvellously adjusted kids.
>
> (Wedell, in interview, 1998, emphasis added)

Here Wedell is reflecting the perennial dilemma in inclusive practices. There are bound to be some elements of a specialist programme which have to be sacrificed. Who decides on such priorities? Wedell suggested 'the kids', which is very much in tune with the 1990s rhetoric of emancipation and empowerment.

Peter Mittler, similarly, was working to integrate children with autistic spectrum disorders from a hospital setting into mainstream primary schools in the early 1960s. Almost 40 years later, he reflected that 'I thought that everyone was doing it, then I realised that it was extremely rare' (Mittler, in interview, 1998).

Both these major influences on special education practices in the UK and beyond claim that they were already thinking *towards* if not *of* inclusion before the term was coined. Although they both acknowledge that it was largely paediatricians who played a key role in their development during the 1960s, in keeping with the dominance of the medical model of disability at that stage, they both became concerned with including young people with disabilities as a matter of course. Mittler, for example, suggested that although he was trained as a psychologist in 'gradualism' – that is, step-by-step rehabilitation of people out of long-stay hospitals into the community – he came to realize, chiefly from US research, that it was more positive and effective to make bold rather than tentative moves forward. In developing 'less faith in the gradualist model', he has come to feel that one of the greatest barriers to inclusion is our underestimation of the potential abilities of those we label as having SEN; by extrapolation, therefore, the very existence of the special educational needs co-ordinator (SENCO) in UK schools is itself anti-inclusive.

Wedell was innovative in understanding in the late 1960s and early 1970s that the child-deficit model was reaching the end of its usefulness, and that it was more practically useful in developing new approaches to observe children in real school settings than in hospitals. Of course, such practice sometimes entailed the loss of apparently valuable resources; Wedell tells of his team's early access to

a marvellous chromium-plated child-study centre. It was beautiful, all purpose-designed. We had moved from a lovely old country house to the centre. It had been designed with one-way vision screens and so on, and I used to do the most fantastically detailed within-child assessment. There was hardly a thing that if you wanted to know about this kid, about his disabilities, that I couldn't tell you about . . . And then when I took over the Ed. Psych. [educational psychology – EP] training course at Birmingham and saw changes occurring, to my great sadness I said, 'We are being absolutely ridiculous. We've been totally sort of swept along by the excitement of having this lovely centre. We are not going to work here; we are not going to have this [sort of] training of EPs.' We moved into schools. But it was a terrible shame.

(Wedell, in interview, 1998)

Examples such as these may suggest something of a pioneering spirit on the part of figures who have later come to be viewed by some as traditional, reactionary and above all perpetuating of a segregated special education. It is important for those examining the development of thinking and ideologies to acknowledge the ways in which key theorists were moving ahead within their *own* time, later to be overtaken by more radical new thinking.

For example, it is not always remembered that before the Education Act 1971, a large number of young people with learning disabilities were legally regarded as ineducable. It is important, therefore, to acknowledge that there were some practices which by today's definitions might be described as broadly inclusive in that they were insisting on the 'educable' status of a group previously denied access to educational provision.

The enduring role of educational psychology in the determination of the developing fields of special, integrative and inclusive education is beyond question. Sheila Wolfendale and Brahm Norwich are educational psychologists who trained in the traditions of Wedell and Mittler, and who have made significant contributions not only to the development of inclusive education, but simultaneously helped redefine and diversify the very nature as well as role of educational psychology in developing practices of working with teachers in the field. Sheila Wolfendale, for example, has strongly influenced the early years support offered by Educational Psychologists in her *All About Me* project (Wolfendale, 1987), while Brahm Norwich has worked on research development in 'cluster' mainstream schools, where teachers have provided peer support in developing their responsiveness to a diverse range of learners and their needs (Norwich, 1993).

What such researchers emphasize is that, although educational psychology generally had a central role in the development of special (segregative) education, there have been many forms of educational psychology, not all of which conform to a stereotype of exclusive practice. There is finally no single, enduring version which – transcendentally, as it were – pervades the history of inclusive education. Rather, the nature and occupation of educational psychology itself has changed, perhaps reflexively with its involvement with special, integrative and inclusive educational expressions of policy.

On this note Brahm Norwich provides a useful reminder that there has emerged a range of psychologies. He highlights the importance of being alert to: 'the tensions within either psychology or medical models (biomedical versus social medical models)'. He calls for more interdisciplinary thinking to include: 'ecological (bio-psycho-social models) or interdisciplinary models which assume interconnections between different levels of analysis' (Norwich, personal communication, 31 March 2000).

## The sociological response

*PC:* I have my doubts, still. I mean it's one thing to have the insight, but quite another to be able to do something about it . . .

*Jim W:* Say more . . . more about insight . . . Doesn't insight lead to change?

*PC:* What I'm saying – what lots of people have said – is that a social critique of special education is . . . what? Well it might be quite right and all that but what difference does it make actually in the classroom, actually to the 30 kids you've got there and you've got to teach? I hear teachers on courses say that, and I think: hmm, yes, well . . . maybe this sort of [sociological] critique is actually disabling to teachers . . .

*JW:* I think you . . . I think you're missing the point of critique . . . It's not about the here-and-now-immediate, but the structures behind which make the here and now so awful . . . it's about vision, too.

(Inclusive Education Research Centre seminar, Sheffield, January 1999)

If the psychomedical perspective saw special educational need as arising from children's own characteristics, by contrast the sociological response sees them as the outcome of social processes. In the previous section we identified some of the contributions of educational psychology to the development of inclusive practices. This section now explores the contribution that a sociological critique has provided, in which the whole rationale for special education, and the professional roles associated with it, were challenged as symptomatic of oppressive processes.

Sally Tomlinson and Len Barton together wrote and edited a number of books which were very influential in developing the sociology of education, and in challenging the segregated special education sector. Both these sociologists located special educational needs in a much broader context than was customary in the work of educational psychologists, and introduced an explicitly political dimension. In 1984, they characterized special education as:

> now a more important mechanism than it has ever been for differentiating between children, and allocating some to a lifestyle that – if not as stigmatised as in the past – will almost certainly be characterised by dependence and powerlessness. In addition, the economic recession in these societies has brought into sharper focus a perennial question in special education – 'How much should be spent on groups who may not be economically profitable or useful in the society?'
>
> (Barton and Tomlinson, 1984, p. 87)

Within the terms of a critique like this it is possible to see the 1981 Education Act, for example, with its structures for formal assessment and statementing, as a clear means of both delimiting public expenditure and maintaining the status quo. The key movement in conceptual focus for this development, then, lies in a concentration on social disadvantage rather than individual deficit. As Barton says of this conceptualization: 'for me inclusive education is not an end in itself, it is a means to an end, and that end is creating an inclusive society ... This is well beyond an issue of disablement; it is about the removal of all forms of oppression ...' (Barton, in interview, 1998).

Sally Tomlinson's 1982 study of the way in which pupils were selected for inclusion in the special schools of the day described as for 'Educationally Sub-Normal (Moderate)' learners, was particularly concerned to illustrate how social class chiefly, as well as ethnicity and gender, were important factors in the process of stigmatization of 'Sub-Normality'.

Tomlinson was one of a number of sociologists who were not primarily interested in special education as a substantive concern, but rather as a location for the exploration of the structures and cultures of difference. Tomlinson's work on special education, then, needs to be seen in the context of a broader concern of sociologists with a platform of issues of inequality and disadvantage, and with the crucial role of the institution in reproducing difference.

Similarly, Bob Lingard – an Australian who has been influential in developing policy in the *Disadvantaged Schools Programme* in Queensland – saw inclusion as about much more than a narrow conception of special educational needs and disability. Lingard says: 'I come out of an interest in kids from poor families and how schooling could be much more inclusive there, and I've been heavily involved with gender issues both at school level and in the development of [government] policy' (Lingard, in interview, 1999).

At the heart of the sociological response are the ideas of the 'vested interests' of professionals and of the institutional 'reproduction' of disadvantage. One of the distinctions to be made between the psychomedical and the sociological approach is in terms of their identification of whose interests are served by a 'special' education. Various sociological commentators started to challenge the previously taken-for-granted assumption that special schools existed benignly, genuine in their concern to serve the interests of children with marked learning difficulties. Critics of segregated systems instead identified other beneficiaries: Tomlinson (1982), for example, was among the first to see the advantages of this system for the medical and psychological professionals with a 'vested interest' in maintaining their own status and power. She argued that: 'the answer to the question "what is" an ESN(M) child or a maladjusted child will depend more on the values, beliefs and interests of those making the judgment than on any qualities intrinsic to the child' (Tomlinson, 1982, p. 66).

Similarly, Tom Skrtic's (1991) work echoed and reinforced an earlier argument made by Tony Dessent (1983) that:

Whatever else education involves it is first and foremost an administrative and organisational system whereby one group of professionals are invested with responsibility for handicapped and 'difficult-to-teach' children. At the same time other groups are absolved from such responsibility. Special education has come to be described and justified . . . in terms of its small teaching groups, special curricula, expertise and methods, but its historical roots lie in the need to remove the responsibility for teaching children with special needs from class teachers in normal schools.

(Dessent, 1983, p. 90)

Much of the work touched upon here is in the form of analysis, critique or 'deconstruction', particularly of what is seen or assumed to 'lie behind' special education. That is to say that some have sought to respond to the medico-psychological legacy by asking some of the very questions about the construction of difficulty posed earlier, and in so doing to seek to find what is hidden, disguised perhaps by systems, structures and a language inherited from earlier psychologically biased trends.

There is no doubt that such broad sociological and political perspectives presented a powerful and provocative challenge to the dominant psychological approaches. Critics, however, might say that they were limited in that the insights they generated related to an analysis of schools and society which offered no practical advice to teachers in classrooms. In the next subsection I shall sketch how these needs of teachers were partially met through what I call here 'curricular approaches'.

## Curricular approaches

*Kathy T:* You could say that [the emphasis on curriculum] really got a boost with the 1981 Act, with its IEPs [Individualized Educational Programmes].
*PC:* And the focus on educational needs rather than handicaps.
*KT:* But it was coming, it had to come, I mean the curriculum revolution of the 70s, all the Stenhouse stuff, it didn't touch well it didn't really touch special education at all.
*PC:* That's right and in fact special ed. curricula were so distinct, so separate because they were all about objectives.
*KT:* I wonder whether . . . I wonder: have we come full circle now, with the National Curriculum and all the specification of the Literacy Hour and so on? Back to objectives in the name of 'Curriculum for All'?
*PC:* Interesting, isn't it, that 'Curriculum for All' was the title of the OU [Open University] books of the 80s, the general title?
*KT:* . . . but very different from David Blunkett's 'Excellence for All'.

(Conference workshop, Nottingham, May 1999)

In the last section I outlined the sociological critique of 'special' forms of education. At the same time as this critique was gathering momentum (in the 1960s and 1970s), there was a related and parallel development of curriculum and teaching approaches which helped to foster a more inclusive school and college culture.

What I am here calling 'a curricular approach' in fact comprises a very broad range of interventions through the curriculum. A highly specific and individual task-analysis programme may be seen as an intervention at the level of curriculum; or else the radical revision of the whole school day can equally be seen as a function of curriculum planning. The point is that each of these interventions depends on different conceptions of curriculum itself. This is partly because, during the period we are considering, the very notion of 'curriculum' was contested and developed. We shall see, then, that curricular approaches to learning difficulties have themselves developed in keeping with the mainstream development of curriculum, and curriculum studies.

> In broad historical terms, there has been a change of conception from *curriculum as syllabus* to *curriculum as cultural scheme*. The whole history of inclusive education in schools and colleges might be plotted in terms of this shift. The shift effectively encapsulates what is meant by inclusion, for if inclusion is essentially about maximizing participation in community and culture, then in schools the medium for this is the curriculum.

I mentioned earlier the 'curricular wasteland' of special education, characterized by Phillip Williams as a garden 'not only secret, but neglected, too' (Williams, 1985, p. vii). Broadly speaking, 'special' curricula up to the era of the Warnock Report were importantly conditioned by two seminal books – *The Backward Child* (Burt, 1937) and *Backwardness in the Basic Subjects* (Schonell, 1942). Burt had identified the 'innately dull' as distinct from those whose 'backwardness was accidental or acquired' (Burt, 1937, p. 606). For these pupils, 'Individual attention . . . should result in progress being so speeded up that all who are not dull as well as back-ward should, after one or two terms, be fit for retransference to the ordinary class' (*ibid.*).

Such a view crystallizes an approach which, for the next 40 or so years, saw the child as needing to be rehabilitated to fit the given curriculum, rather than the curriculum in any way adapted to meet the child's needs. Schonell (1942) went on to confirm and refine Burt's distinction, introducing the notion of 'improvable scholastic deficiency (which) . . . may characterise dull, normal or supernormal pupils' (*ibid.*, p. 61). And in terms of actual teaching responses, since 'typically such deficiency was confined to a single school subject', '*treatment for the condition* was through individual or small group short coaching sessions arranged at frequent intervals rather than in full-time backward classes' (Golby and Gulliver, 1985, p. 139, emphasis added). In their critical discussion of these years,

Golby and Gulliver go on to say that such ideas

> were offered to the world at the very time when those educational notions which culminated in the 1944 Act were being formed. An idea of retardation which was based on psychometrics fitted well with education which would be given in accordance with 'the age, ability and aptitude of the pupil.' It buttressed the idea that ability was measurable, that children could therefore be grouped and taught in homogenous units, and that the curriculum for each of these units was distinct . . . Burt and Schonell's focus upon reading and number confirmed teachers in the epistemic divisions which were still believed to be necessary.
>
> (*Ibid.*)

Golby and Gulliver conclude:

> Thus, when in the late 1940s the first remedial centres were set up, they were received with open arms by teachers . . . [This development] however, diverted attention from the 'normal' curriculum itself. *So long as remedial provision was made – an ambulance service in a system which was prone to accident – the curriculum could remain a static entity.*
>
> (*Ibid.*, emphasis added)

I have quoted at some length from Golby and Gulliver's paper because it points up richly the conception of curriculum as essentially a form of treatment that lay so deeply at the heart of 'special' and 'remedial' education. It was a conception which was to endure for many years and which powerfully maintained and reinforced the separateness of mainstream and 'special' provision.

Arguably, the first really noticeable development of curriculum in special education came with the use of objectives in meeting learning difficulties. Generally speaking, the use of objectives – and particularly behavioural objectives – in the UK followed their burgeoning use in the USA in the 1950s. One of the earliest and most important influences on UK developments was the Hester Adrian Research Centre at Manchester University – importantly under Peter Mittler's guidance – and projects such as the Education of the Developmentally Young (EDY) (McBrien, 1981) which the centre set up. However, perhaps the best known of these behavioural objective approaches to teachers in special education, is that articulated in Mel Ainscow and Dave Tweddle's (1979) Coventry-based *Preventing Classroom Failure: an objectives approach.* Parallel approaches are present in the Special Needs Action Plan (SNAP) (Ainscow and Muncey, 1981) and programmes like DataPac (Akerman *et al.*, 1984). What is chiefly characteristic of these approaches is an 'assess: teach: assess again' approach. Reason, Farrell and Mittler (1990) comment that such

> assessments assume that the curriculum can be drawn up as a hierarchy of target skills and knowledges to be mastered. At the top of the hierarchy is the basic subject area . . . which has targets . . . Each of these targets is broken down into teaching aims . . . and these are further divided into pupil objectives which

state what pupils have to do to demonstrate that they have mastered the teaching objective.

*(Ibid.,* p. 1026)

Three final quotations here will serve to point up the orthodoxy which an objectives approach to learning difficulties came to have during this period. In 1978 the Warnock Report actually defined the curriculum in terms of 'four interrelated elements', which are '(1) setting of objectives; (2) choice of materials and experiences; (3) choice of teaching and learning methods to attain the objectives; and (4) appraisal of appropriateness of the objectives and the effectiveness of the means of achieving them' (DES, 1978, p. 206).

In the same period, Ainscow and Tweddle (1979) spoke of the assumption in their work 'that they are special schools because sophisticated teaching methods and techniques are used in them . . . In fact, [the behavioural objectives approach] is the kind of system which should be operated in a special school or unit if it is "special" in more than name only' (*ibid.,* p. 105).

Finally Mittler (1981), in a prospectus written in the same period, titled 'Teacher Training for the 21st Century', listed the skills and knowledges that special educators would need, which included 'proficiency in the specification of behavioural objectives, goal setting, task analysis, programme writing' (*ibid.,* p. 10).

---

In terms of the historical development of inclusive education, such a view of the role of objectives in curricula may now seem naive. There is also no doubt that this view of the 'special' curriculum as not much more than a set of teaching plans helped maintain its separateness from 'regular', mainstream systems. However, it is also possible to see in these activities two important contributions to

- the beginnings of a direct connection of assessment with curriculum, and a reflexive relationship between them in the teach/assess/teach cycle
- the emerging recognition that educational difficulties are not exclusively something 'within' the learner, but are importantly related to instructional conditions.

---

### Curricula for all?

These insights, however, are still far removed from a radically different strand of curricular approaches. This is a strand which owes its development more to social movements than to psychological constructs. It is also a strand which is far more explicit about the comprehensive school values which drive it. As Alan Dyson says of this 'route to inclusion', it is a

> tradition which derives from post-war egalitarianism and is closely related to the comprehensive movement. I'm not certain that this is the same as [the sociological critique of] Tomlinson and others. A number of commentators, however (Tony Booth principally) relate their vision of inclusion (however labelled) to comprehensive education. My own focus likewise has been less to do with disability *per se* than with issues of disadvantage and marginalisation affecting a large minority in the education system.
>
> (Dyson, personal communication, 2000)

If, during this period of the 1970s, the curriculum of 'special' education can be characterized in terms of objectives, curriculum in the mainstream was occupied with radically different issues and practices. In contrast with what could be seen as the *contraction* of curricular thinking in 'special' education, mainstream development was rich with expansion. Fresh insights into the nature and process of learning:

- threw into question notions of 'innate' or 'static' ability
- challenged assumptions about the nature and acquisition of literacy
- began to point up the vital role of learners themselves in the 'construction' of knowledge
- indicated new ways of grouping knowledges which broke with some of the traditional subject boundaries
- suggested changes to pedagogic organization which had traditionally grouped learners by ability.

These, and other, features of the period found their expression in emerging programmes such as the Schools Council Humanities Curriculum Project aimed at 'average and below average' pupils, and which were built around interactive methods like small-group discussion. Most importantly, however, all such developments must be seen as expressions of the major ideological shift during this period from elitism to equality of opportunity, and thus from the categorical sorting out of children at age 11 to the espousal of a comprehensive education system. Such a system depends reflexively on the principle of a common curriculum.

---

It is arguably the curriculum which always stood – secure as a Berlin Wall – between mainstream and segregated special provision; it was the possibility of mediating that curriculum, and the means of its delivery, which enabled 'integrative' education; and it is still the curriculum on which the success of any truly inclusive initiative rests.

---

Many of the important foundations for inclusive practices, then, are to be seen as arising from a strong ideological commitment to comprehensive schooling, and a form of curriculum which would truly realize it. Arguably one of the most important contributions made during the 1980s and 1990s was that of the Special Education team at the Open University. Recruited initially to develop SEN courses within the Psychology Section of the School of Education, the team early developed a radical and characteristic conception of inclusive education which was essentially continuous with comprehensive ideology. The team significantly relocated itself within the Curriculum Studies Section, and rapidly developed courses which turned their backs on traditional, psychologically led enquiry. These courses owed their character rather to the ideas of Lawrence Stenhouse (1975) and the Centre for Action Research in Education (CARE) at the University of East Anglia, with their emphasis on teacher- and action-research. They arguably represent the first major operational expression of inclusive schooling in UK university departments of education.

Pre-eminent in their widespread audience and effect is the suite of books developed by the OU team, chiefly Tony Booth, Patricia Potts and Will Swann, with titles (from as early as 1983) such as *Integrating Special Education* (Booth and Potts, 1983) and the series Curricula for All (1987) which comprised three books whose titles say a great deal about the ideological as well as pedagogical programmes which they propose:

- *Preventing Difficulties in Learning* (Booth, Potts and Swann, 1987)
- *Producing and Reducing Disaffection* (Booth and Coulby, 1987)
- *Including Pupils with Disabilities* (Booth and Swann, 1987).

Similarly oriented, the latest series of readers (to support Course E829: Developing Inclusive Curricula) is called Equality and Diversity in Education.

But there is more to the generic OU approach than an ideological commitment to comprehensive community schooling. For the very nature and structure of the teaching materials themselves represent a quite particular, and no less ideological, commitment to a conception of learning which questioned *what* students were required to study and *how* evidence was presented and evaluated, and to *what* ends. Answers to these questions were framed in a mode of critical enquiry which owed much more to mainstream curriculum studies than to any tradition of a 'special' education. Tony Booth reflects on the development of the 'shape' of the team's first course, E241: Special Needs – Education 'around three questions:

- What's going on [in Special Education]?
- How do we make sense of 'what's going on'?
- What *should* go on?'

He then goes on to relate a particular ideological commitment to an equally particular conception of enquiry:

> I was reading stuff about life history at the time. And I was very occupied with – and still am – the question: How d'you – anyone – learn from [your] experience? How can students learn from experience? The task was – and is – to develop studies that don't depart from your own experience . . . [I was impressed by] the whole freeing up of method that was exercised by CARE, the liberation of method was so refreshing . . . which I linked up with the philosopher of science Feyerabend's *'Against Method'* and it was that liberalising of method that was terribly influential; but not just the liberation of method, but of epistemology, of the whole epistemological foundation of methods of enquiry. That was the other side to the development of E241 – the use of case study [methods] – [we] battled hard for acceptance of them as a legitimate approach to study . . . so for students to get a book which was almost entirely case studies of people's experience, that felt like a big breakthrough.
>
> (Booth, in interview, 2000)

Booth's point, of course, is that this shift from predominantly quantitative to qualitative methods was of particular significance in an area (of 'special' education) which had for so long been dominated by psychometric and generally positivist approaches.

The Open University initiatives were supported and reflected by related work elsewhere which problematized the role of the curriculum, and schools themselves, as creative of difficulties. Among others, key publication of this time and tone include:

- Paul Widlake's (1984) *Beyond the Sabre-Toothed Curriculum*, an eloquent attack on the moribund curriculum of 'remedial' education
- Hazel Bines's (1986) *Redefining Remedial Education*, which articulated a new, supportive role for teachers in providing access to the curriculum for all
- John Sayer's (1987) *Secondary Schools for All?* which carefully laid out strategies for making the school a 'resource for the community' where 'special needs can be met *only* within the context of the whole school'
- Tony Dessent's (1987) *Making the Ordinary School Special*, a template for the development of continuous, comprehensive, community education.

It is worth noting in concluding this section that the conceptions of curriculum to be found in the above derive from the territory of inclusive, mainstream practices, and were nowhere to be found in the parallel literature of 'special' education. Thus, for example, Wilfred Brennan's book *Curriculum for Special Needs* was published at roughly the same time as most of the above (1985) but carries no reference whatever to the work and ideology of people like Stenhouse (1975) or Carr and Kemmis (1982).

> What I have called curricular approaches to inclusion, however varied, have as their central identity the understanding that what we ask an individual to do – how we ask it and when – will directly determine his or her success as it is experienced by them, and as it is defined by their community. If this is a rather obvious truism, then it is one which has often been overlooked by curriculum policy-makers. And it is the one which – arguably more than any other educational structure – has maintained a disconnected 'special' and 'mainstream' structure.

In the conclusion to *Theorising Special Education*, Catherine Clark, Alan Dyson and Alan Millward ask whether it is 'time to move on'. This call follows their

> contention that it is now time to 'reconnect' special education. We are advocating a theoretical position which emphasises the connection between special education and fundamental educational issues. That position calls for an analysis of special education from a perspective that is broader than the concerns of special education, that is historical and that is situated in the complexities of particular structures and practices at particular times and places. [Such a position promises to move] on beyond the repetitive and sterile arguments within which [special education] has latterly become
> trapped. (Clark, Dyson and Millward, 1998, pp. 172–3)

In the next section I shall sketch a key emerging position in the development of inclusive education which operates precisely from a reconnection of 'special' with 'fundamental educational issues', and continues the identification of inclusion with comprehensive ideals.

### School improvement strategies

*Barbara N:*we've been talking about this [effective school movement] as though it's one thing, but it really isn't so, is it?
*PC:*... important differences between school improvement like for position in the league tables, number of A–Cs and all that, and school improvement for the good of all ... the IQEA [Improving the Quality of Education for All] stuff and other ...
*DJC:*Yes when we talk about the effective school you've got to ask 'Effective at what? Or for who?'
*PC:* Or ... what would an 'effective', a truly effective Comprehensive school look like? ... Roy Hattersley gave a talk here last year and he said one of the things he said was 'There's no such thing as a Failing Comprehensive, and do you know why? Because there's still no such thing as a Comprehensive'.
(Teacher INSET workshop, Sheffield, February 2000)

In 1991, Mel Ainscow edited and published a collection of papers called

*Effective Schools for All*. Based substantially on the International Special Education Conference of the previous year, the book brings together what – in the usual context of 'special' education – is at first sight an unusual confection of writers. But the significance of the inclusion of 'mainstream' commentators such as Neville Bennett and David Reynolds is found easily in the book's explicit attachment to school improvement (as the primary means of realizing inclusion). Describing his own professional development, Ainscow cites David Hopkins, Lawrence Stenhouse, Rob Walker and John Elliott – among others – from 'the action research movement', writers 'who argue for cooperative inquiry'; and 'evaluators who base their work on the notion of naturalistic inquiry' (Ainscow, 1991, p. 12). From these and other influences, Ainscow identifies six common strands to characterize a prospectus for his emerging work:

1 Forms of inquiry are used that encourage teachers to examine particular events or processes as a whole and in their natural settings.
2 The design of the inquiry is seen as being emergent; that is to say, the directions and forms of an investigation are decided upon as information is collected.
3 The teacher is seen as the primary 'instrument' for gathering information, using natural methods of information-gathering such as observation and discussion.
4 Wherever possible inquiry is seen as a collaborative process involving colleagues and pupils.
5 Through processes of data analysis and interpretation, theories emerge from information that is collected. This is usually referred to as 'grounded theory' in that it is seen as being grounded in the data.
6 Accounts are usually presented as case studies with, where possible, some attempts to suggest tentative applications of the findings to other settings.

(Ainscow, 1991, p. 13)

The connection with the writers, ideas and concepts of the previous section – on curricular approaches – will be obvious. What is novel, however, is the explicit bringing together of such methodologies both with notions of learning difficulty and with the mainstream policy concerns of the 1990s. Above all, what Ainscow is working out here – and through subsequent work such as *Improving the Quality of Education for All* (Hopkins, West and Ainscow, 1996) – is a *vision of inclusive education as simply given with effective comprehensive schooling*.

It is really only during the last decade that 'school effectiveness' as a 'movement' or 'school' of thought became part of the educational currency. It is all the more difficult to trace the connections I identify here because, as Booth (1998) reminds us, it is necessary to step outside the special and inclusive literature, in order to learn from 'mainstream' ideas. When he calls for the 'removal of boundaries' (*ibid.*, p. 88), he does so in order to incite an interconnectivity between researchers, disciplines and ideas. If

A central premise of Lawrence Stenhouse's work was that: 'Curriculum development involves bringing practice in classrooms and teaching plans closer together through an evaluation by teachers' (Stenhouse, 1975, p.77). Such work brought the notion of teachers exploring and developing their own curricula to the fore, and represented a 'devolution of power' (McNiff 1988) of curriculum evaluation. Action research, curriculum research and developmentand teacher research were tools and processes which, in the hands of creative teachers, forced the differentiation of curriculum materials and the evolution of curriculum 'entitlement'. Essentially, this set of approaches could be characterized as focusing on schools and curricula as directly related to – and sometimes productive of – learning difficulties. In a strong sense, notions of inclusive education are vitally related to these conceptions of the curriculum, extending as they do to include school and college ethos, institutional culture, and the ways in which behaviour management is maintained and monitored; and, of course, the role of pedagogy in creating inclusion and exclusion.

we pursue the notion of the disconnected nature of various educational research strands, we can find an example in the separately developed themes of special and inclusive education and 'school effectiveness'. The relatively recent development of school effectiveness in relation to the field of SEN is evidenced by the writers in Clark, Dyson and Millward (1998) who comprehensively discuss key theories and recent thinking in SEN and inclusive education. Is it significant that while some attention is given within the text to the concept of school effectiveness, there is no reference to the term in the index of the book (which normally conveys both its architecture and major political concerns)? In parallel, in *The Intelligent School* MacGilchrist, Myers and Reed (1997) report school effectiveness developments, and cite examples of practice within the sphere of special education. But they, too, omit terms such as 'SEN' or 'inclusion' from their index. This may seem a small point, but it underscores Booth's call to look outside a narrow field of enquiry. There is much to be gained in the development of educational thinking by going beyond one's front door, and 'taking cuttings' from other people's gardens. I give the disconnection some space here, because I want to emphasize yet again how difficult it can be, when studying aspects of special and inclusive education, to trace connections of new thinking and practice.

## Disability studies critique

*CT:* It's ironic really – people talk to me about the 'struggle' for disability rights, but what do they know?
*PC:* About living with the fight for. . .
*CT:* About living it? Not theorizing it – living it!
*PC:* There's the point about the whole context in which we think about education – when we're thinking about disability . . .
*SM:* No, you see, it's the isolation of disability that's the problem – and so is the isolation of education a problem . . .
*CT:* Oliver is right when he talks about the connection between health, housing . . .
*SM:* Yes and care, support – work with families . . .
*PC:* And the stuff about the connections between educational and social policy.
(PhD student supervision session, Sheffield, March 2000)

As with the previous perspectives, there are clearly a number of differing accounts which might be seen to make up a broadly homogenous critique. You will see from Colin Barnes's and Mike Oliver's different accounts (in Section 2) that there is no single orthodoxy to what I have for ease of reference here called the 'disability studies critique'. What I wish to show, however, is something of the vital and conditioning influence which a number of scholars have brought to debates around inclusion from *outside* education – as it were – and which has directly affected the development of schools' policies.

Disability studies is of course an almost entirely separate discipline from educational studies, and as such its contribution to debates on inclusive education are unique. This is an important point, for the disability studies movement cannot therefore be said to hold a *curricular* brief as such. For this very reason – that is, its 'outsideness' from education – its contribution to educational debate may be arguable, with both strengths and weaknesses. One of these strengths, though, is the way that it can relate specific issues of social inclusion, and inclusion in employment and housing, to educational inclusion within a 'big picture'.

One of the earliest and most influential expositions of the disability studies critique in the UK is to be found in Mike Oliver's paper 'The social and political context of educational policy: the case of special needs' published in 1988. In it, Oliver shows how 'Educational policy has not developed separately from other initiatives in the area of health, housing, social security, family support and so on [and that] much can be learnt from studying the relationships between educational and social policy' (Oliver, 1988, p. 13). Oliver characterizes these social policies in terms of four ideologies. Respectively, these are expressed: as humanitarian response, as social investment, as the outcome of conflict between competing groups and as social control. Oliver's main argument is that initially, disability was perceived as an individual problem; it then came to be seen as a social construction and, finally, it is beginning to be perceived as a social creation . . . [and] largely due to the growing power of disabled people, the definition of disability as a social creation is now gradually being accepted as the most appropriate one.

*(Ibid.)*

Although theorists like Oliver are concerned with issues of the creation of disability, special education has only been a small and incidental element of their critiques. Oliver, in particular, applied a Marxist analysis to his discussions on social and economic developments. His interpretation of progress remains significantly different from that often presented by those offering either a psychology or curricular approach, which have tended to suggest that there are areas of development and positive achievement despite obstacles. Oliver's evaluations, on the other hand, tend to the pessimistic. Interviewed in 1998, Oliver commented:

> maybe there are marginally a few more children with physical impairments in ordinary education . . . and a few less with educational and behavioural problems in ordinary schools, but at the end of the day that is only at the margins and the power structures remain virtually unchallenged and untouched, and I think there are obviously a number of barriers: there are political barriers, economic barriers . . . there are professional barriers. Teachers still do not concede, and even the most enlightened and 'right-on' teachers who would have no trouble in recognising oppression on the basis of class or race or gender, would still be happy to say 'I am not taking a blind child', or 'I am not taking a deaf child into my class, and that is not a political issue, that is a resource issue' . . . and I think those kinds of oppressive attitudes have changed remarkably little over the last 20 years or so.

Oliver concluded his 1988 paper with a quotation from John Fish's 1985 paper, 'Community, co-operation, co-partnership'. Actually, in Fish's paper there comes together – though surely not to everybody's satisfaction – a credo which seems to reflect equally on insight from disability critique and from a curricular understanding of learning difficulties. Fish says:

(i)   Although disabilities and difficulties may be different, and their nature, effects and the needs which result from them should be studied, the handicaps which stem from them have many common characteristics.

(ii)  Handicaps are determined by society through its laws, norms and institutions and not by disabilities.

(iii) Handicapping effects result from the nature of the situations met by individuals with disabilities and difficulties in education, social circumstances and employment.

(iv)  The degree to which situations are handicapping is determined by the community, its attitudes and its provision for individuals who form part of it.

(Fish, 1985b, p. 5)

I think it very significant that Oliver openly endorses John Fish's credo. These principles, Oliver (1988, p. 29) says, 'clearly represent a significant shift' from the individual and social constructionist definitions and practices given with the Warnock era and culture. However, it seems clear that Oliver's injunction (of 1988) remains unrealized in the year 2000: 'The development of a pedagogic practice based upon the definition of special educational needs as a social creation is . . . an urgent and essential task over the next few years' (Oliver, 1988, p. 29).

## Conclusion: powerful coalitions?

By looking 'back' through the disability studies critique at the influences of the psycho-medical model, the sociological response, curricular approaches and school improvement measures, is it possible to look *forward* to the emergence of a more homogeneous response to inclusive schooling with individual learners rights to inclusive education – as well as needs for individually appropriate education – at centre stage? More specifically, I wonder, is there some recent convergence of thinking about inclusion, about what it is – or should be – and about how it will be best achieved? Perhaps this is just a hunch of mine which comes from spending time researching this book, and talking with the people who appear in Section 2. Perhaps also it is a hope. In any event, what I think there is evidence of is a convergence of energies of different sorts in the project of inclusion. Let me give two examples of this:

1 The project shared by Jennifer Evans, Alan Dyson and Klaus Wedell, which is reported in *Collaboration for Effectiveness: Empowering Schools to be Inclusive*. Here there is a combination of differing backgrounds, perspectives and talents which perhaps ten years ago could not have been imagined.
2 The *Index for Inclusion* (Booth *et al.*, 1999), published by the Centre for Studies in Inclusive Education (CSIE), and the outcome of a particularly fruitful collaboration between two very different researchers, Tony Booth and Mel Ainscow as well as the CSIE.

I suggest that these developments among others reflect something of a trend. Taken generally they represent some powerful emerging coalitions in inclusive research and development in at least three ways:

1 *Epistemic*: by which I mean the attempts to bring together different forms, or disciplines, of knowledge, such as psychology and sociology. It should be clear from my earlier discussion that this particular combination of studies is particularly significant given the history of special and inclusive education;
2 *Methodological*: by which I mean the bringing together and justification of a mix of research methods, styles and ideologies, to some extent

reflecting the epistemic synergies (mentioned above).

3 *Institutional*: by which I wish to point up the increase in collaboration not only between individuals, but also necessarily between the institutions for whom they work (and this, of course, includes organizations such as the Joseph Rowntree Foundation and local education authorities. (I should also suggest that there is some perceptible increase not only in inter-institutional work, but also in *intra*-institutional collaboration in the name of inclusion: there are now quite a number of university departments of education in the UK with 'dedicated' and substantial research and teaching centres in inclusive education, as well as those in social studies departments, for example).

Perhaps the most salient example of a current 'powerful coalition' is to be found in the shared work of three very different individuals, with very different backgrounds and from very different institutions. Mel Ainscow, Tony Booth and Alan Dyson first published work some years ago and have gone on to collaborate quite prolifically. You will see from Section 2 how different are the 'routes to inclusion' which each has taken. Yet they appear currently to evidence a collaboration of which one can truly use the (often clichéd) notion of 'synergy'. However it is evaluated, the effect of three key figures in inclusive education working in concert, bringing to this particular work their years of scholarship, is an example of the complex weave over time of differing trends and practices.

For me, they also exemplify a form of curricular approach which might be summarized in this way:

[If] . . . curriculum is placed at the centre of 'special needs' enquiry, then special needs provision will necessarily move nearer to the centre of curriculum issues, no longer marginalized but the very touchstone and proving point of coherent, sensitive and moral curriculum planning for all. [On] . . . the part of teacher and researcher alike, this curricular approach will call for:

a. The framing of problems in the *whole* context in which they are noticed; such a frame will recognise the relevance of the aims and organisational structures of the *particular* institutions quite as much as the needs, motivations and intentions of all the individuals under study.

b. A theoretical framework which is capable of taking account of such complex interrelations by drawing on a *variety* of sociological, psychological and other theories rather than exclusively relying on any one of them.

c. A systematic recognition of the *experience* of participants – teachers, pupils and parents – in order better to understand and interpret teaching and research situations.

d. The empirical monitoring and documentation of learning events by both teachers and researchers leading to critical self-evaluation and appropriate revision of methodologies.

(Clough, 1988, p. 337)

## The (almost) final word: Le Bourgeois Gentilhomme

In conversation with a philosopher, the main character in Molière's play *Le Bourgeois Gentilhomme* – Monsieur Jourdain – is surprised and delighted to be told that he has been speaking prose all his life without knowing it! This was the image and structure that Klaus Wedell chose to use when we interviewed him in 1999; he referred to his own position as

> a *bourgeois gentilhomme* situation . . . where what's-his-name, I've forgotten his name says, 'I didn't realize that I was talking [prose] all the time' . . . I started being an educational psychologist in 1964 . . . in Bristol . . . [and] I became concerned about children who weren't developing language and who were deaf and we hadn't got any provision for them and we said 'Well . . . what are we going to do with them?' and the natural thing was to set up a unit in a nursery school, and we purposely chose a room that had a door into the main room and the door was left open at certain parts of the day and progressively the kids would, move towards the door, stand by the door, stand outside the door and I wasn't thinking of . . . being inclusive I was just . . . that was what I felt education was about then. So in a sense, that is why I am saying 'I didn't realize that I was talking 'prose' all the time'.

What is Wedell claiming here? That he was 'talking *inclusion* all the time', whatever it was actually called at the time? That the move to *integrate* was – for its time – an essentially *inclusive* thrust? Peter Mittler could be seen to be making a similar claim about his early work to include children with autistic spectrum disorders, reflecting that 'I thought that everyone was doing it, then I realised that it was extremely rare' (see p. 13, this chapter).

If this is so, then perhaps you could equally argue that an inclusive drive is to be found in the 1944 Education Act (which 'included' pupils previously outwith the educational system) or – surely? – the 1870 Act, marking the beginnings of mass popular education. Perhaps the metaphor of 'casting the net ever wider' describes this general move. And is 'inclusion' therefore not a recent phenomenon but rather an evolving set of ideas immanent in the historical development of educational institutions?

How do you set about deciding the answers to these questions? Is this 'revisionism'? And who says so? Who has 'the final word'? I hope that some questions will be answered through the Profiles and Reflections of Section 2. But of course, the *final* word will be yours: it is for you to decide how these claims and my views fit with your other reading and your own thoughts, experiences and analyses. To help you start to do this, I have appended a Workshop Exercise to this section. I hope that this throws some light on your own 'route to inclusion': travel hopefully!

# Appendix: reviewing the journey

This workshop exercise has been constructed as a tool to help you reflect back upon what you have read, and on your other reading of literature in the field in order to construct your own map of the routes to inclusion. You may wish to complete the table provided as part of your own private study, or within your own student group. If you do the latter you will, no doubt, find that you engage in much critical discussion and questioning. Section 1 has suggested five major routes in the development of inclusive ideology and practice. Before you leave this section and move on to engage with the finer details of some of the people who have contributed to the construction of this map, you may wish to review the journey so far. In Section 1 you have explored with me some of the territories of inclusive education, tracing five major routes identified as:

1  the psycho-medical legacy.
2  the sociological response.
3  curricular approaches.
4  school improvement strategies.
5  disability studies critique.

Clearly there has been no neat progression from one idea to another and as Figure 1.2 illustrates (p. 9), one influential 'school' may continue to contribute to thinking and practice while newer, perhaps more popular, approaches begin to dominate. It is the case that all five of the major routes to inclusion that I have discussed here impact upon the way we now see inclusion – both in society and in educational practice.

Table 1.4 begins to extract some of the ideas included in this section in order to summarize the key strands within each 'route'. Looking at the table you will see that some summary points for the psycho-medical model have been inserted. Using the material available throughout Section 1, add the summary points for the other 'routes'. There may well be some cells which cannot be completed; for example, if there were no specific legislative contexts to speak of, that cell would remain blank.

**Table 1.4** The five major routes in the development of inclusive ideology and practice: a summary

| | The psycho-medical legacy | The sociological response | Curricular approaches | Effective schooling | Disability critique |
|---|---|---|---|---|---|
| Form of knowledge/ epistemology/ discipline | Positivist Natural sciences Psychology | | | | |
| Key concepts | Deficit | | | | |
| Source of difficulty/ problem viewed as | Individual pathology | | | | |
| Locus of intervention | Individual 'treatment' | | | | |
| School setting implied | Segregated/ special school | | | | |
| Dominant period of influence | ? | | | | |
| Significant legislation and policy contexts | 1944 Education Act | | | | |
| Dominant research methodology | Quantitative Measurement | | | | |
| Other? | | | | | |

# Section Two

## *Journeys in inclusive education:*
### *Profiles and reflections*

Peter Clough and Jenny Corbett

# Introduction

This is the central part of the book. It leads from Peter Clough's section on some of the routes to inclusive education, into a set of writings *of* and *about* some of the writers who have contributed to the debates. It also provides an important *bridge* between Peter's Section 1, and Jenny Corbett's Section 3, where students' own thinking and writing is shown engaging directly with theory.

The section is made up of what we have called Profiles and Reflections, presented alphabetically. The Profiles have been written by us using transcribed interview data, and each of these accounts has then been read and approved by its subject. The Reflections, on the other hand, are firsthand accounts provided in writing by other subjects.

We have selected our sample of writers to include people who have been practising mainly as academic teachers and researchers for many years and who can offer a rich, historical perspective on the dramatic changes and developments they have seen in their lifetime. These influential writers provide a most valuable opportunity for students in this field to learn about the evolution of ideas and theorizing. They show how there are conceptual staging posts along the way which may have been revolutionary for their time in social history, although they may now appear outdated. We think it is really important to listen to those who have 'travelled' far and have much to share, for any apparently new concept like inclusive education always has a complex and evolutionary growth. Some of its origins may be found in the most unlikely places!

The sample of authors here includes those who would not wish to align themselves to any specific theoretical stance, preferring to remain eclectic. Others are forcefully attached to one particular ideological position, while some will take elements from perhaps two related areas. This reflects the reality among any group of writers on a particular area like inclusive education. It is important for students of this field to maintain an attitude of openness to keep yourselves open to the fact that there are few *ideologically pure* theorists. Writers who draw from a number of different theoretical sources may be equally strong – if not stronger – within the academic rigour of their debates.

The range of authors included here is not comprehensive in scope, neither is there any strongly purposive selection. We are well aware that many major contributors to debate are not included (particularly from 'outside' educational debates and outside the UK). However, what we still hope to have achieved in this section is the bringing together of a range of different views and experiences. Many of these accounts also richly demonstrate the lived relationship between the – apparently distinct – *personal* and the *professional*. Many of these accounts show how systematic thought, analysis and theorizing are quite continuous with and expressive of the wider life experience. It is important to reflect that all those who develop distinct and influential perspectives are informed to a greater or lesser degree by what has happened to them, their professional observations and their opportunities to grow and develop. This is true for this sample of writers, as it is true for any reflective practitioners who are linking analytical thinking to their own experience of practice.

# Profile

## *Mel Ainscow*
### *University of Manchester, UK*

### Sample texts

*Preventing Classroom Failure: An Objectives Approach*
(Ainscow and Tweddle, 1979)

*Teacher education as a strategy for developing inclusive schools* (1993)

*From Them To Us: An International Study of Inclusion in Education*
(Booth and Ainscow, 1998)

### Major influences

I can identify a number of key people, for example Dave Tweddle, David Hopkins, Susan Hart and Tony Booth, who I have worked with and who have been major influences on my thinking. I am still proud of the work Dave Tweddle and I did in that school in Walsall because I think it was genuine and authentic. The work I have done with my Cambridge colleagues took me very close to schools and I learned about the richness of being close to practice on a day-to-day basis. It is about trying to make sense of life's experiences in a professional sense and very much valuing the role of other human beings in that process.

In the second part of the 1980s when I went to Cambridge I had moved from being concerned with particular children to being concerned with contexts. Getting involved in school effectiveness and then school improvement was very important to me at that stage. There really was a kind of changing perspective towards wanting to look at schools and what was and wasn't working and listening to teachers.

A major influence has been the work I've done with UNESCO and the Enabling Education Network which has led me to look at countries, where resources are really stretched, importing failed approaches from Western countries which I find a very worrying tendency. Part of the theory of the Enabling Education Network is for people in the southern hemisphere to learn from each other as, where you have experiences of people working in very poor environments you often find they are doing creative things on the ground, which are not recognized and valued because of this deference to Western technology. I have fallen into the same trap of acting as a kind of courier of technology from the West and realizing that it does not fit. I think this is what takes me to the notion of 'collaborative enquiry' which is a key influence on my practice.

## Quotations from sample texts

Obviously teachers evaluate the various methods they try, but this process tends to rely heavily on subjective impressions and is rarely documented or recorded in any systematic way. Instead, evaluation usually depends on a teacher trying out something with a class one year, and then if it *seems* to work, using it and, perhaps, improving it the next year with another group of children. Setting work at the right level, therefore, depends upon analysing the skill to be learnt into carefully graded steps. Such a teaching programme will then be a matter of leading the child with learning difficulties through the predetermined steps, allowing time for each stage to be thoroughly mastered before proceeding to the next. The ojectives approach provides a framework for making this process logical, systematic and explicit and is consequently less dependent upon the indefinable personal qualities and intuition of the teacher.

(1979, p. 25)

At this point in my argument it is important to recognize that reconstructing the special needs task in terms of school improvement and teacher development is likely to lead to a challenge to the status quo of schooling and teacher education. At a political level it addresses questions to those who create and administer policy; and at the professional level it presents challenges to individual teachers and those involved in their education. Specifically, it requires many to suspend their existing beliefs and assumptions about the origins and nature of educational difficulties in order to consider alternative perspectives. Instead of the traditional search for specialist techniques that can be used to ameliorate the learning difficulties of individual pupils, the focus must be on finding ways of creating the conditions that will facilitate and support the learning of *all* children.

(1993, p. 205)

We argue that a field of special education can be redefined, in part at least, using the concepts of inclusion and exclusion. Students placed in special education categories are some of those who have been subject to exclusionary pressures in schools, and their categorisation itself has often contributed to the process of exclusion. The attempt to engage such students in curricula appropriate to their interests and attainments and foster their participation with others can be seen as fostering their mainstream inclusion. For us, however, a *redefinition* requires us to go further than to change words, to merely relabel traditional special education with the phrase 'inclusive education'. It involves detaching a concern with inclusion and exclusion from a particular history of special education, concerned with the identification and remediation of student deficits and defects. It requires that we see students with disabilities and those who experience difficulties in learning as part of the diversity of the student population, subject to a wide variety of inclusionary and exclusionary pressures. It means that we have to resist a division between 'us' and 'them', the normal and abnormal students and the use of the euphemistic categories, such as 'learners with SEN', which obscure such a practice.

(1998; pp. 243–4)

## Reflections on inclusive education

The key time for me in terms of making sense of my learning about inclusive education was in Coventry where we worked on the model I had brought with me from my special education background, that of devising individual responses to children in regular schools.

Inclusive education is really a process of people enquiring into their own context to see how it can be developed and it is a process of growth. It is a social process which engages people in trying to make sense of their experience and helping one another to question their experience and their context to see how things can be moved forward.

I am engaged in the development of practice. I work with schools. I work with teachers. I work with LEAs. I think that I am very good at working with people and I, therefore, make things happen or help to make things happen because of that skill. I see myself essentially as a teacher. All the best things I have done have involved me working with groups of people all the time, where we have developed some initiative to make something happen or overcome something. I seem to have a skill in helping people to think together, to overcome problems, to be energetic.

I have a transformative approach to inclusion which involves asking how can we actually transform the education system, such that it is more capable of developing its capacity to reach out to all learners in a way which suggests it is an ever ongoing process that never ends in that sense. My current preoccupation is to ask how can people in a given context be helped and help one another to explore their context in relation to barriers to participation and learning and how can they be creative in overcoming them. I think the concept of 'special educational needs', particularly as it is seen in this country, becomes another barrier. I don't think it has a productive contribution to make to the inclusive education agenda. If anything, it is one of the major barriers to moving forward.

## Links with different theoretical models

I think there is a degree of fragmentation and separation among the different theoretical models. I think there is a greater need to bring together people who are interested in marginalized groups and to explore the connections. What I have instinctively been wanting to say is how do we use the different perspectives together to collectively engage with making an educational system which is more responsive. There is fragmentation between 'special needs' and 'general school improvement' or 'educational for all', in international terms, and then within special education between the special needs and disability people. The whole fragmentation process is in itself one of the major barriers to progress. But, of course, there are vested interests as well.

I think I would avoid at all costs using the term 'special needs'. I know you can't but, I mean, it wouldn't be part of my actual engagement with either myself or with close colleagues really. I think I am much more driven by concepts of 'education for all' and comprehensive education in a way. An issue that has always been a sort of pain in the side for me is the whole issue of disability. I welcome being challenged by the likes of Richard Rieser or Finkelstein and so on, who come with a strong disability angle. I find it quite useful to have their challenge, but my natural interest is more broadly about how schools cater for differences really. I find that just concentrating on disability is actually very limiting as an agenda in a way. I understand their argument that, if we take the broad view that I want to take, they will continue to be the most marginalized group. I think there is a healthy kind of intellectual attention paid to that now.

# Reflection: Inconclusive education?
# Towards settled uncertainty

## Julie Allan
### University of Stirling, UK

## Sample texts

Foucault and special educational needs: a 'box of tools' for analysing children's experiences of mainstreaming (1996)

*Actively Seeking Inclusion: Pupils with Special Needs in Mainstream Schools* (1999)

The aesthetics of disability as a productive ideology (forthcoming)

Recently, while marking exam papers, I came across one script in which the student had referred, not to inclusive education, but to *inconclusive education*. I initially mulled over my homicidal thoughts, feeling that having got only halfway through a pile of 300 scripts, this was too much. But then I began to realize that this person was right and that what we are striving for is, indeed, inconclusive. My own research, involving listening to pupils' accounts of mainstreaming, suggests that inclusion is never complete, but always in process, which contrasts with the static picture that is often presented of inclusion being *done* to individuals.

This story is itself inconclusive and narrates my trip (meaning stumbling rather than the more apparently rational and coherent journey) towards a state of settled uncertainty. John Keats referred to this state as 'negative capability . . . [when one is] capable of being in uncertainties, mysteries, doubts, without any irritable reaching after fact and reason' (1817). I have selected three texts which illustrate different points along the way. The first of these is 'Foucault and special educational needs: a "box of tools" for analysing children's experiences of mainstreaming'

(Allan, 1996); second is a book, *Actively Seeking Inclusion: Pupils with Special Needs in Mainstream Schools* (Allan, 1999); finally I refer to a paper which I presented to an International research colloquium (Allan, forthcoming). I will try to show how the production of these texts has been influenced by a number of theorists outside special education and disability, but most obviously by the work of Michel Foucault, and by literature and disability arts. What follows is not a neat and tidy story, but a messy and fragmented series of stumbles. The single element of continuity and synthesis comes from disability studies, through the social model's constant influence on my teaching and research practice, and in the disability arts movement, which uses a range of art forms as a political tool against disablism.

## Achieving 'negative capability': a story of buckets and a box of tools

My first brush with uncertainty came as a graduate student, embarking on my first PhD and attempting to get to grips with the endless paradigms, epistemologies, ontologies and methodologies – all of which seemed unbelievably obscure. I finally went to see a friend and brilliant scholar, Andrew Sinclair, who had no formal supervisory relationship with me, but who, I hoped, would offer consolation. His room was its usual mess, so I sat on an upturned bucket and wept: 'I'm never going to understand all of this.' He threw his head back and laughed, then said 'I'll have a word with God.' His point was that we could never hope to grasp the whole picture 'but it could be great fun trying'. That particular PhD went into the bucket and a few years later I started, and this time finished, the PhD which was to kick the bucket of certainty and closure.

The discovery of Foucault's 'box of tools' (1977, p. 208) promised a way into understanding disability and inclusion through discourses. The starting point, following the social model of disability (Finkelstein, 1980; Oliver, 1990), was that disability and inclusion was socially constructed and these processes were revealed in what people said and wrote (both formally and informally) about them. In my own 'box of tools' article (Allan, 1996), I explored the relevance of archaeology and genealogy, two of Foucault's methodologies for studying power and knowledge, to special needs and argued that we had to 'add Foucault and stir' (Shumway, 1989, p. 161), that is adapt it creatively, rather than faithfully, to this context. While undertaking the research, however, I became interested in Foucault's final phase of ethics, in which he gave individuals considerable scope to resist the power exercised upon them. That was particularly exciting because of three things which were emerging from the data. The first was that the pupils with special needs were transgressing boundaries placed on them by others (through attitudes, etc.) and were *actively seeking inclusion* (Allan, 1999) Second, the mainstream pupils were operating a kind of mini-governmental regime which was mostly supportive of inclusion. Finally, the teachers' practices sometimes impeded inclusion, but this seemed to arise from a clash of discourses – between teachers' professional discourse of need and pupils' discourse of desires – and seemed open to resolution. I began to feel optimistic about the project of inclusion, so ended the book with an account of inclusion as an ethical project for all of us – pupils with special needs, mainstream pupils, teachers, parents and researchers. This project was definitely not envisaged as one of closure, but of creating openings and of sustaining inclusion *in process*. Writing about inclusion in a way that conveyed momentum was tricky and Foucault (who remained a structuralist thinker) was limited in this respect. Help, however, came from the anthropologist Homi Bhabha (1994), and his analysis of the 'in-betweeness' of identity, and from Derrida's notion of 'undecidability' (1972, p. 72). Joyce and Becket also provided some of the language to convey the simultaneous ambiguity and ambivalence of inclusion processes.

## Ideology and the aesthetics of disability

After the book, I needed to get my teeth into something big and ideology happened to come along. An argument had been brewing in the USA between the inclusionists and the special educators, with both sides using ideology as a weapon with which to beat the other. An excellent paper by Brantlinger (1997) was the basis for the meeting of an International Colloquium on Inclusion in Rochester, USA in June 1999. What began for me as a paper about ideology became an account of the impossibility of knowing it (Derrida, 1998; Zizek, 1994). Through Zizek, I discovered Sloterdijk's (1987) version of kynicism, which attacks piety by 'pissing against the idealist wind' (p. 103) and pursues a kind of 'healthy narcissism and self affirmation, which sets out to 'laugh in the face of the impudent demands of such morose societies' (*ibid.*). I was particularly pleased to discover that the Eastern European novelists have also succeeded in making ideology limp. For example Kundera (1986; 1991) and Hasek (1973) have unravelled idelology, by demonstrating its internal irrationality and taking us to 'the horror of the comic' (Kundera, 1986, p. 104). It is, however, the disability arts writers (e.g. Aaron, 1997; Napolitano, 1998 and Wade, 1987) who have gone furthest by creating an aesthetics of disability which puts ideology to work in a more productive way. What they have established is a king of eye-poking genre, which forces non-disabled people to look at their own disabling practices. The discourse which speaks here is characterized by desire, respect for difference, and this, I feel, is where teachers, schools and teacher education have to go. The most voluble discourse at present, however, is that of the school effectiveness and school improvement 'movements'. The aesthetics of disability needs a strong voice to speak against the weighty discourse

of effectiveness and improvement, but this following extract, on which I
end my story, will hopefully indicate that it is more than up to the job:

> *I am not one of the*
>
> I am not one of the physically challenged –
>
> I'm a sock in the eye with a gnarled fist
> I'm a French kiss with cleft tongue
> I'm orthopedic shoes sewn on a last of your fears
>
> I am not one of the differently abled –
>
> I'm an epitaph for a million imperfect babies left untreated
> I'm an ikon carved from bones in a mass grave in Tiergarten, Germany –
> I'm withered legs hidden with a blanket
>
> I am not one of the able disabled –
>
> I'm a black panther with green eyes and scars like a picket fence
> I'm pink lace panties teasing a stub of milk white thigh
> I'm the Evil Eye
>
> I'm the first cell divided
>
> I'm mud that talks
> I'm Eve     I'm Kali
> I'm The Mountain That Never Moves
> I've been forever     I'll be here forever
> I'm the Gimp
> I'm the Cripple
> I'm the Crazy Lady
>
> I'm the Woman With Juice

(Wade, 1987, p. 408)

# Reflection: a disability studies perspective

*Colin Barnes*
*University of Leeds, UK*

## Sample texts

Disability studies: new or not so new directions? (1988)

*Cabbage Syndrome: The Social Construction of Dependence* (1990)

*Disabled People in Britain and Discrimination: A Case for Anti Discrimination Legislation* (1991)

Qualitative research: valuable or irrelevant? (1992)

Foreword, in *Disability Politics: Understanding our Past, Changing our Future* (1996a)

Disability and the myth of the independent researcher (1996b)

Several factors influenced my particular approach to disability studies. I have lived with disability all my life. Both my parents had accredited impairments. My father had a congenital visual condition and spent his entire working life in sheltered workshops of one form or another. My mother experienced periods of severe emotional distress and was diagnosed a 'schizophrenic' when I was quite young. She spent long intervals in psychiatric hospitals. And because I have a similar condition to my father's I attended 'special schools' until I was almost 12 years old.

Although I hated special school I have only fond memories of my childhood. My parents did not consider themselves disabled but part of the 'respectable' working class. My father was a socialist and a committed union man and my mother a Tory; a difference which only became apparent during elections. They taught me many things including the importance of 'independence', accountability and integrity; I owe them a great deal.

My concern for social and political issues was stimulated further during the cultural upheavals of the 1960s and 1970s. I had worked in the catering industry since leaving school but decided on a change of direction. Hence, in the mid 1970s I started going to night school in preparation for a career in social work. Here I was introduced to sociology, labelling theory and Marxism. This started me thinking seriously about disability and discrimination, the role of special schools, and the problems faced by disabled people and other socially disadvantaged groups.

In the early 1980s I began working in local day centres with young disabled people and then went on to teacher training college. From here I went to Leeds University, as a mature student, to study sociology and sociological insights into society's treatment of people labelled disabled. Although at that time disability was relatively low down on the academic agenda, the staff at Leeds, especially Geof Mercer, Carolyn Baylies and Ray Pawson, were helpful and supportive.

As a student at Leeds I came across Vic Finkelstein's *Attitudes and Disabled People* (1980) and Mike Oliver's *Social Work with Disabled People* (1983). These books were especially significant as they introduced me to the social model of disability and the idea of a disabled people's movement. I became actively involved in the movement in 1989 when I began working for the British Council of Disabled People (BCODP). Through my involvement with BCODP I met various leading figures in the disabled people's movement including Vic, Mike, Jane Campbell, Rachel Hurst and Ken and Maggie Davis, and various others too numerous to mention here; all of whom have, to varying degrees, influenced my thinking on disability and related issues.

## Quotations from sample texts

Academic development all too often resembles a never ending conflict between memory and forgetfulness. As as consequence, important insights and ideas are sometimes abandoned, or conveniently forgotten, only to reappear at some later date in some new guise or form. Moreover, reinventing the wheel but calling it something else is an all too common feature of scholarship in the latter half of the twentieth century.

(1988, p. 577)

all physical impairments have psychological implications and all intellectual impairments have physiological consequences.

(1988, p. 578)

the need for a radical reappraisal of societal attitudes and social policies regarding children and young people with impairments has never been more acute. Existing policies which successfully disable children and adults with impairments by not providing them with the confidence, practical and intellectual skills, and opportunities necessary to live outside institutional settings are no longer simply morally reprehensible, they are likely to prove economically disastrous.

(1990, p. 203)

Institutional discrimination is evident when the policies and activities of public and private organisations, social groups and all other types of organisation in terms of treatment and outcome result in inequality between disabled people and non-disabled people . . . It incorporates the extreme forms of prejudice and intolerance usually associated with individual or direct discrimination, as well as the more covert and unconscious attitudes which contribute to and/or maintain indirect or passive discriminatory practices within contemporary organisations.

(1991, p. 3)

To understand fully the extent and complexity of the discrimination experienced by disabled people in modern Britain an understanding of history is critical.

(1991, p. 11)

Analytically the experience of impairment is not a unitary one. The range of physical, sensory and intellectual abilities within the disabled community is vast. Some people experience a lifetime of disability while others only encounter it later in life. Having an impairment does not automatically give someone an affinity with disabled people, nor an inclination to do disability research. The cultural gulf between researchers and researched has as much to do with social indicators like class, education, employment and general life experiences as with impairments. Emancipatory research is about the systematic demystification of the structures and processes which create disability, and the establishment of a 'workable' dialogue between the research community and disabled people in order to facilitate the latter's empowerment. To do this researchers must learn how to put their knowledge and skills at the disposal of disabled people. They do not have to have impairments themselves to do this. Indeed over the last ten years I have met many people with impairments who are unsympathetic to the notion of disability as social oppression and many able bodied people who are.

(1992, pp. 120–1)

For me . . . the politics of disablement is about far more than disabled people; it is about challenging oppression in all its forms . . . It is impossible, therefore, to confront one type of oppression without confronting them all and, of course, the cultural values that created and sustain them.

(1996a, p. xii)

University based researchers are not free of external considerations and controls. To suggest otherwise is to misrepresent social research in the 1990s. Furthermore, in my view to maintain the myth of the 'independent researcher' within the context of disability research – or any kind of social research, for that matter – can only exacerbate the gulf between researchers and research subjects – the very opposite of what is needed.

(1996b, p. 243)

# Profile

## Len Barton
### University of Sheffield, UK

### Sample texts

*The Politics of Special Educational Needs* (1988)

*Disability and Society: Emerging Issues and Insights* (1996)

*Inclusive Education: Policy, Contexts and Comparative Perspectives*
  (Armstrong, Armstrong and Barton, 2000)

### Major influences

When I became appointed as a teacher of woodwork and swimming at an
adult centre for people with learning difficulties, this was my first
encounter in any serious way with disabled people. Two factors influenced
me into taking that job. I worked in a small firm and the only future for
me within the building industry was to start my own firm and I didn't
want to do that. That was one factor in the decision. The second was a
religious factor, that these people needed somebody like me. It was a
Christian-informed pressure.

My understanding about disability has changed fundamentally over
time and this has been due to several influences. In particular the writings
of disabled scholars such as Oliver, Abberley, Barnes and Morris, and
specific friendships that I have established with disabled individuals. A
further influence has been my involvement in sociology of education and
the friendships and working relationships I have been able to establish
with others within the discipline. Being able to understand disability
within a wider context of inequalities of relations and conditions of society
has been one of the benefits of a sociological approach.

## Quotations from sample texts

The question of the 'politics of special educational needs' has to be defended and I wish to argue that it can be viewed in the following ways. First, there needs to be a relentless systematic effort on the part of all interested parties in attempts to influence governments in relation to enhancing the lives and opportunities of people who are labelled in this way, particularly as the vast majority of these children and young people are, or will increasingly be, from lower socio-economic backgrounds. Secondly, there is an essential revelationary role to be undertaken in highlighting the ways in which various policies and practices, including the assumptions and expectations underpinning daily interactions, contribute to the creation of handicaps and the resultant suffering which follows. Thirdly, in endeavouring to connect the personal with the political, it is crucial that the thoughts of those with disabilities are made public and that these become the basis for political alliances and endeavour.

(1988, p. 7)

An 'emancipatory' approach to the study of disability entails engaging with several key issues. For example, establishing relationships with disabled people, listening to their voice and, in my case, being white, male and non-disabled, raises the following sorts of questions:

What right have I to undertake this work?
What responsibilities arise from the privileges I have as a result of my social position?
How can I use my knowledge and skills to challenge forms of oppression disabled people experience?
Does my writing and speaking reproduce a system of domination or challenge that system?

These questions form part of a complex and unfinished series of concerns.

They are important aspects of a challenging learning experience which is both disturbing and enabling. What does it mean for a sociologist to listen to the subjects of study? What are the important issues for establishing and maintaining relationships with disabled people, when part of the sociological task involves critically engaging with participants' perspectives? How does the emancipatory practice deal with the conflict of interests the sociologist finds herself in over participants' ignorance, prejudice and reactionary motivations and behaviour? Part of the sociological imagination involves a healthy scepticism and a desire to get beneath surface features to the deep structures of social relations and experience. What does this mean for the sociologist who seeks to take a supportive stance in relation to disabled people?

(1996, p. 5)

Demands for inclusive schooling should concern not only the 'rights' of disabled children but are also part of a wider critique of that which constitutes itself as 'normal'. In the absence of such a critique, notions of 'opportunities' and 'rights' rest upon an understanding of 'normality' that reflects the partial self-interest of dominant social groups in our society. Our own starting point is that inclusive education is inextricably linked to a political critique of social values and practices and the structures and institutions which they support. The analysis of 'value' must explicate the role of education in the production and reproduction of different values, including the 'value' invested in children and young people as commodities and the representation of this value in terms of 'special' needs. In struggling for the implementation of inclusive practice we are engaging in a political process of transformation.

(2000, p. 11)

## Reflections on inclusive education

It is a political issue because of the way in which it may be connected to wider inequalities in society. Special education can be seen, historically, and may be increasingly seen in the future, to be serving a wider interest of society, in a world in which the economies and opportunities for occupations are becoming less and less for particular groups of young people. I am thinking here particularly of black Afro-Caribbean and some white working-class young people in some of our inner cities who are going to find the world increasingly difficult with regard to employment. So, there is a way in which special education can be seen as a means of control, as a means of legitimating the dominant forms of discourse and interests of a given society, in particular a world of marketization, com-petitiveness and selection. It makes sure the system continues as smoothly as possible by removing those difficult, objectionable and unwanted people to other spheres. It is, however, often justified on the basis of being in their interests, of meeting their needs.

## Links with different theoretical models

My approach has been rooted in socio-political perspectives, linked to disability politics, to sociological and political science traditions. There clearly has also now been an increasing disability politics influence coming through in all sorts of ways and that's taking a variety of interesting divergencies, between a structural emphasis, and the politics of identity. A sociology of impairment is developing where the issue of the body is being engaged with in a much more fundamental way than hitherto.

I think the book on *The Politics of Special Educational Needs* meant a lot to me. It was important to the field at that point in time. The book *Disability and Society* was also very important in that it brought together disabled and non-disabled sociologists to debate and discuss disability issues. It contains a wealth of insights, ideas and topics for further examination.

However, the most exciting and I think effective engagement in my academic life, has been with the creation of the journal *Disability and Society*. It is now the world's leading journal in disability studies and is published seven times a year. To be involved in this development, to work with so many talented and committed people, to establish an outlet for the dissemination of cross-cultural insights and questions, and to help develop a greater understanding of the manifold forms of disabling barriers and ways of challenging them, has been a very real privilege. This clearly has also contributed to my own re-education.

# Reflection

## Douglas Biklen
### University of Syracuse, USA

### Sample texts

*Achieving the Complete School* (1985)

*Schooling without Labels* (1992)

*Communication Unbound* (1993)

*Contested words, contested science* (Biklen and Cardinal, 1997)

'I am intelligent': The social construction of mental retardation (Biklen and Duchan, 1994)

Foreword to *Schooling Children with Down Syndrome* (in Kliewer, 1998)

My introduction to disability came abruptly, a few months into graduate study in social policy. I participated on a research team investigating living conditions in large state institutions for the so-called 'mentally retarded'. These facilities housed anywhere from 1,200 to 6,000 residents, children as well as adults, classified according to U.S. definitions at the time as profoundly retarded, severely retarded, moderately retarded and mildly retarded.

My training was in ethnographic research, not in special education, and this may have helped me to be able to see what I saw. At one institution, the official brochure described a habilitation agenda:

> The goals which we are striving for at our institution are to provide shelter, food, security, sympathetic care and understanding for each retarded individual entrusted to us ... We offer opportunities for the retardate to develop physically, mentally, emotionally, socially, and spiritually to the full limits of his potential. For none is it a dungeon of oblivion and neglect.
>
> (Biklen, 1977, p. 45)

Then, at the same institution, one of our research team observed:

> We walked over to the women's infirmary. Here I saw women tied down in
> chairs, women tied to chairs that were tied to the walls. I heard moaning as I
> walked through the day room, and the stench was overwhelming ... I saw a
> woman tied under a restraining sheet. 'How long has she been there?' I
> inquired. The attendant answered, 'A long time.' I asked, 'Do you get her out
> every so often?' The attendant smiled, 'Yes, we have to rub her down every two
> hours. That's the law.' I asked another question: 'How long will she be under
> that sheet?' Our guide responded, 'For the rest of her life.' 'Why?' I asked. 'She's
> a head banger,' he said.
>
> (Biklen, 1977, p. 45)

At another institution medications were the favoured means of control:

> I saw the nurse come over to a three-year-old boy who was sitting quietly in
> his crib. She was going to give him a cup of liquid tranquilizer. They boy fought
> her off, but then lost the fight and was forced to drink the medicine. Before she
> had arrived, he had been sitting quietly. As she walked away from the crib, he
> was crying loudly. When I asked why he was given the medication, she told
> me that he would get too 'Hyper' without it.
>
> (Biklen, 1976, p. 51)

It was hard to know what aspects of institutional life were the worst: the
restraints, tranquillizers, the stench of faeces, the absence of educational
programmes, loneliness, being barked at ('Get in line; shut up!' 'I said get
in line. Be quiet, I said.' 'Just shut up. Shut up and say your prayers.') or
barren living quarters? Boredom must have been overwhelming:

> I asked, 'What do the children do all day?' The attendant responded, 'Right
> now we're in the waiting period.' 'What's the waiting period?' ... 'It's the hour
> before meals when they wait for their food,' she replied. I was curious by now
> ... 'What do they do when they're not waiting for meals?' To this she
> responded, 'Mostly sit around, look at each other and sleep.'
>
> (*Ibid.*, p. 71)

I was interested in how people got to such places and, through a series
of studies came to understand that families often placed their children in
institutions because they had been rejected at the pre-school and school
door. In other words, it wasn't really that particular aspects of certain
disabilities determined who would be institutionalized, it was more a
function of social policies and discriminatory practices. Later, I would
come to see a similar practice in school placement, what I termed 'the
myth of clinical judgment,' noting that whether or not a child would be
included or excluded from mainstream education depended not so much
on the nature or degree of a child's disability but on where the child lived,
and the prevailing practices of that jurisdiction.

Interestingly, while all of my work to that point reflected a disability
rights (as in civil rights) perspective and a sociological critique of
institutional 'care', very much in the tradition of Goffman's *Asylums*, I had

not yet considered a serious critique of the diagnostic categories themselves, especially 'mental retardation'.

Naturally, from an ethnographic vantage point, I was open to the idea that disability was socially constructed and that at any given time there were a range of available social understandings of what disability meant. But I was not yet really acknowledging the implications of this perspective through my writing; so it must not have been clear to me. My line of work shifted from the institutions to schools, where I observed that what happened to students reflected particular orientations and models of schooling. Typically, students profited to the extent that they had teachers who advocated and strategized for them within an otherwise segregationist system – I termed this the 'teacher deals' approach to mainstreaming or integration (Biklen, 1985). There were other more segregated versions of 'integration', what I termed 'islands in the mainstream' (e.g. special classes in regular schools). A preferred approach was what I termed 'unconditional mainstreaming', which involved teachers, administration, parents and the school community fashioning schools to serve the range of students. But I still really had not addressed a serious critique to dominant conceptions of disability, especially to mental retardation.

Increasingly, my work shifted to listening to parents whose intimacy with their children allowed them to see abilities that I and others were missing. In the book *Schooling without Labels*, I quoted one mother of a son she adopted from an institution. His speech was limited, he was labelled autistic and severely retarded, but she saw him as a complex, intelligent child:

> He was sitting on the couch quietly with a book open, just crying. I couldn't imagine what was happening. He had never had quiet moments like that at that point or at least very rarely. I just looked and didn't say anything. He was looking at Burt Blatt's book, *Christmas in Purgatory* (1966 exposé of abuse in mental retardation institutions). He looked up and said 'big house.' It was like he recognized that this was about where he had been. I sat down and we went through the book together. He just cried. At this point he had very little language. It was just amazing to me . . . He has shown me time and time again, 'Don't underestimate me and don't judge me by your outside perceptions.'
>
> (1992, p. 57)

This mother saw complexity and also her son's budding social justice perspective.

This mother's approach to her son is one of expectancy, of searching for dialogue. It is a perspective that I've come to call 'presuming competence'. For me, this is a useful replacement for the deficit notion of 'mental retardation' (or for 'intellectual disability') which as a social construction does not have any good educational purpose. The presuming competence notion correctly places responsibility on educators to find ways of connecting, of teaching and of learning from the other person. I'm not sure when I first started to act on this notion, perhaps it has been with me for a very long time. I've written about it in numerous locations now (Biklen, forthcoming; Biklen, 1993; Biklen and Duchan, 1994; Biklen and Cardinal 1997) but most recently in the foreword to Kliewer's book on inclusion and Down syndrome:

> A number of years ago I came across a quotation on a pamphlet published by a self-advocacy group in Melbourne, Australia, that read, 'Don't think that we don't think.'
> [. . .]
> The ... statement poses two fundamental questions ... How do you know what someone knows? ... What are the consequences of presuming incompetence?
> [. . .]
> Painfully, in some instances, we see obvious evidence of ability either missed or explained away, even *in* classrooms where students with (disabilities) ... attend with nondisabled students. Reassuringly, we also see scenes of students with (disabilities) ... engaging in intellectual work in schools, also in typical classrooms ... being appreciated and supported for their contributions.
> [. . .]
> Presuming incompetence allows educators to dismiss students' learning, to overlook abilities and contributions, and to see nothing but failure. In contrast, presuming competence allows the educator to see the other person as a peer; it requires a democratic outlook, a commitment to justice. The presumption of competence allows education to begin.
>
> (Biklen, 1998, pp. ix–xi)

# Reflection

## Tony Booth
### *Canterbury Christchurch University College, UK*

## Sample texts

Demystifying integration (1981)

Introduction to the series: Curricula for All (1987)

Stories of exclusion: natural and unnatural selection (1996)

Inclusion and exclusion policy in England: who controls the
  agenda? (1999)

## Major influences

I was born in 1944 towards the end of the war. There were strong views
about social justice in my household, growing up in a Jewish household
when most Jews in Europe had suffered so terribly helped to develop in
me that sense that I had to be aware of the potential within people for
destroying each other – to be aware of the changes that made this less and
more likely. My father had been very active in the fight against fascism in
the 1930s and had taken a few beatings from Mosley's thugs as well as the
police.

It was important to find out what was the right thing to do, and then
to try and do it. You have to look to see what's right because it actually
matters.

Writers who have influenced me most are those who have a strong
moral and political commitment whether inside education like Brian
Simon or the writings of Nawal El Sadawi, and Primo Levi, people who
you take as your guides, your markers for your thinking, people who help
me to keep my 'footing'.

I do not see myself as working within a field of special education any
longer but on issues of educational inclusion, participation and exclusion.

I see the maintenance of a field of special needs education as itself exerting a selective pressure on the education system and so fit uneasily perhaps in this project.

## Learning from experience

I gained insight into segregation in my first year of working as an educational psychologist in 1970/71. My postgraduate course had taught me a  patter for meeting with parents and discussing whether or not their children should be in a special school. But those parents were telling me quite different things; they didn't have a patter, but they were telling me their real concerns. So after having this kind of exchange with three or four parents I stopped listening to myself and started listening to them instead, and that immediately made me question the kind of decisions I was making. I stopped sending children to special schools and administering intelligence tests.

It was around that time that there were concerns about the over-representation of black students in special schools, so I did a survey in the LEA and there was an over-representation there, but I also found that the black pupils were by and large the 'star' pupils in the special schools. So I showed my colleagues what was going on and there was a complete lack of interest. In another authority I remember being shouted at by a colleague for suggesting that integration implied the closure of special schools. It was through those sorts of experience that I began to question the whole idea of special education.

I worked with a parents group around 1977 documenting their fight for inclusion. They all had children with Down syndrome and their reasoning was impeccable, so much more articulate and carefully thought-out than the authorities they were fighting . . . who would come out with the most astounding comments like 'Well, the trouble with you is you've got an over-cooked mongol'. The professionals were coming out with invective and the parents were coming out with reasoned and assured arguments about why their children should be part of the mainstream.

At that time, too, the Campaign for Mental Handicap were very powerful in their opposition to segregation in long-stay hospitals and in special schools, particularly people like Ann Shearer and Peter Beresford.

Maureen Oswin is a particular hero of mine.  For some reason she didn't have this inhibition which came between what she saw and what she told herself she saw. She started reporting on the conditions in which young children 'with learning difficulties' were kept in hospitals like the one in which she worked. She exposed some really dreadful practices on children's wards and was told: 'if you say anything about this your chances of promotion will be gone forever'. I asked her recently about her experiences and she said she'd had support from Jack Tizard in her work, who with Elizabeth Anderson was beginning to open up discussions about integration of students with impairments in the early 1970s. But when she talked to another senior academic in special education about what was happening, she was told 'It's not the time to speak out'. This person had witnessed the same conditions in hospitals as part of an official government body producing reports that were kept secret. He had said nothing.

## Schools, curricula, policies and cultures for diversity

When I joined the Open University at the end of the 1970s, I started putting together ideas about 'Schools for All', the title of a pamphlet by Peter Beresford and Patience Tuckwell, which did not segregate students on the grounds of disability and attainment with the development of a comprehensive community education system. We fought out the content of our first course. I took the view that integration should be an assumption of a course; a moral position. This is a common enough stance now but then it provoked quite a reaction from some people who cheerfully voice their commitment to inclusion now it is safe to do so. I wrote an article documenting the espousal of a commitment to integration in official documents which claimed that this was happening while at the same time special school numbers were mushrooming. Some people did not want to believe the contradictions or the figures. I felt that a commitment to integration or inclusion in principle involved a commitment to putting principles into practice – a demonstration of sincerity.

My colleagues and I took our course out of the psychology discipline group and located it in curriculum studies. Territorial disputes for the ownership of a field of inclusive or special education still continue. But we sought our understanding of the field in the experience of teachers and students, professionals and policy-makers rather than on the shelves of the 'disciplines'. We shaped that first course around three questions: What's going on (in special education)? How do we make sense of 'what's going on'? And: What should go on? – that was quite a breakthrough because it involved accurate reporting rather than wishful thinking, including an understanding of the reality and effects of power relationships. We supported our work with case studies. There was official unease about what we were doing but the students flocked to the courses.

Many people contributed to the thinking then. Jo Campion's recording of the voices of disabled women was powerful. Understanding other sytems, in the USA, Norway and Italy was a considerable source of lasting ideas. There was Lise Vislie's work in Norway linking comprehensive and special education and Richard Weatherley's exemplary documentation of education reform in Massachussetts. I have maintained this comparative strand including a particular involvement in South Africa as well as other countries.

The work has continued, trying to keep in mind C. Wright Mills injunction to combine perspectives on individuals, social systems and societies in order to understand any area of human activity. The more detailed exploration of 'curricula for all' and 'curricula for diversity in education' came in the 1980s and 1990s. More recent work is emphasizing the significance of cultures in promoting or preventing sustainable change in education institutions as reflected in the use of 'cultures' 'policies' and 'practices' as the three dimensions of the *Index for Inclusion* (Booth *et al.*, 1999).

## Quotations from sample texts

I have defined integration as a process of increasing children's participation in the educational and social life of comprehensive primary and secondary schools. Clearly this definition can be applied to all children, not only those currently regarded as having special needs.

I was prompted to examine the facts which form the basis of this article because many people were expressing views which were at variance with my own experience. I heard of fears that large numbers of handicapped children were being 'dumped' into ordinary classrooms without appropriate support; that there was a 'bandwagon' of integrationists who were pushing through plans for integrated education without careful preparation. My own experience of working as an educational psychologist for a local education authority and of watching special schools open and fill had indicated a trend in the reverse direction ... The passing on of myths is a less mysterious process than their creation ... In my more cynical moments I am led to doubt the sincerity of many, including those who write government reports who argue for the integration principle. For, logically, the belief that handicapped children should be educated alongside others in principle entails a desire to see this occurring in practice ... In my even more cynical moments I see the espousal of the integration principle coupled with a suggestion that integration is actually occurring as a neat way of promoting the opposite process. For if integration is occurring we don't have to promote it. If we don't promote it the forces which have led to an increase in segregation can continue without hindrance.

(1981, pp 288, 289, 298–299)

We are concerned, then, to examine the ways in which schools can respond to and reflect the diversity of their pupils. We have come to see how both an integration principle and a comprehensive principle can be elucidated by being linked to a principle of equality of value. In schools which operate according to such a principle, attempts are made to reduce the devaluation of pupils according to their sex, background, colour, economic or class position, ability, disability or attainment ... If however we are to see pupils who gain Oxbridge entry as of no greater value, as no more worthy of congratulation, than pupils with severe mental handicaps, then this has far-reaching consequences for what happens in schools and for how we perceive social inequalities outside them.

(1987, pp.viii–ix)

One might have thought that the very use of the word 'exclusion' to replace the words 'suspension' and 'expulsion' in describing pupils sent home from school for breaches of discipline . . . would push us to connect 'disciplinary exclusion' and other exclusionary events and processes in schools. Exclusion also has an interesting opposite: inclusion. In the 1990s 'inclusion' or 'inclusive education' has begun to replace 'integration' . . . I have written elsewhere about the dangers of the internationalisation of concepts such as 'inclusion' which detach our understanding from local cultures and histories . . . but I have recognised, the advantage offered by the semantic invitation to reflect simultaneously on inclusion and exclusion. Yet it is uncommon either for those who work on 'disciplinary exclusion' or for those who work on exclusion by 'special need' to put their heads together or reflect on the way these sets of processes are compartmentalised in their minds.

(1996, pp. 22–3)

I define inclusive education as the process of increasing the participation of learners within, and reducing their exclusion from the cultures, curricula and communities of neighbourhood centres of learning. I have begun to experiment with calling this project 'inclusion/exclusion' to keep these dimensions at the forefront of our minds. It is concerned with the careful fostering of a mutually sustaining relationship between local centres of learning and all members of their surrounding communities. It is about giving learners an equality of regard irrespective of their background, gender, ethnicity, sexuality, disability and attainment . . .

A narrow view of inclusion concedes the inclusion agenda to central government, and hides the exclusionary force of a competitive system of education in which schools are seen as failing corner-shops or successful supermarkets. It restricts our thinking and blunts our critique. We cannot include others, or ourselves, in education unless we speak our own words.

In writing about inclusion/exclusion I try to keep in mind an audience which includes both the countries of the North and the South. This choice of imagined surveillance is a reminder of supra-national exclusionary forces and a need to be explicit about the context of my work. It involves adopting a comparative perspective, and I suggest that this is the paradigmatic discourse within social science, challenging us to reflect on our assumptions and parochial concepts. It demands that we move between vantage points, so that the strange is made familiar and the familiar strange. It requires a recognition that academic exchange involves people at the apex of one set of cultural formations reaching out to those at another, within or between countries. However, a belief in a shared global academic discourse seduces many into thinking that they do not need to make this effort. What is produced in such a state of mind is a linguistic fog in which language becomes detached from the contexts which hold its meanings.

(1999, pp. 78—97)

## Disputing the inclusion territory

Some continue to want to make inclusion primarily about 'special needs education' or the inclusion in education of children and young people with impairments but that position seems absurd. When I'm in a mosque in East London which has narrowly escaped a nail-bomb, and I'm consulting with the Management Committee of the mosque about how they feel about the educational participation of Bangladeshi students, who can tell me that I'm not involved in something that's fundamentally about inclusion and exclusion? Nobody could say I'm not, but at the same time there's an ideological cloud that reinvents the primacy of disability in understanding inclusion.

If inclusion is about the development of comprehensive  community education and about prioritizing community over individualism beyond education, then the history of inclusion is the history of these struggles for an educational system which served the interests of communities, and which does not exclude anyone within those communities. It needs to trace its roots within community and comprehensive education as well as within the struggles for rights of women, black people, gay people and disabled people and other groups who's participation is made conditional and vulnerable. The history of inclusion doesn't take you back to special education.

# Reflection

## *Peter Clough*
### *University of Sheffield, UK*

## Sample texts

Bridging the gap between 'mainstream' and 'special' : a curriculum problem (1989)

*Making Difficulties: Research and the Construction of Special Educational Need* (Clough and Barton, 1996)

*Articulating with Difficulty: Research Voices in Inclusive Education* (Clough and Barton, 1998)

Crises of schooling and the 'crisis of representation': the story of Rob (1999)

## Influences

I am struck by the number of people I know whose initial experience of working in special education seemed, as it were, accidental. Yet at the same time I don't really believe in this 'accidental' account; without being fatalist or therapist about it, I think that most people's involvement in 'special' education is – or becomes - knit fairly densely with their 'personal' lives and there's usually some (psycho)logic to it. Certainly I can see a distinct weave of personal and professional threads in my own career.

I did my first degree in the late 1960s and you couldn't be impervious to the mix of passion and propaganda that characterised the social and ideological life of the late 1960s and early 1970s. My work in mainstream and special schools during the 1970s; my work with teachers in initial training through the 1980s; my experience of becoming and being a father throughout the 1990s (and I shouldn't omit the 'facts' of my own childhood and the experiences of being a somewhat 'deviant' son); and

65

my current work with disabled and non-disabled Masters and PhD students – all those things come together in my work and in my writing.

I am conscious of my very strong personal reaction against the 'categorization' of human experience – be it by sociologists, psychologists, whoever. I also find it problematic to acknowledge particular kinds of authority – particularly in terms of the epistemological. So acknowledging this – in terms of my own work and discipline – I tend to think more in terms of the arts as knowledge bases rather than social, natural or physical sciences.

Apart from Merleau-Ponty's phenomenology, there is no one theoretical model which I link with solely. But if I were to name one name in the field of education, it is surely Lawrence Stenhouse. It is impossible to encounter the work of Stenhouse and not see curriculum in a different light – the teachers' ownership of curriculum, action research, curriculum inquiry – democracy in learning in classrooms. And within that comes the political realization of Comprehensive education – itself an inclusive project. The development of Comprehensive schooling was a vision of equality, of an inclusively educated society – which lasted some 20 or so years until the systematic dismantling of that began in the 1990s.

My interest in how life proceeds as a narrative now drives and influences my work in special and inclusive education. I write research stories that draw upon – and help me to explore – my work with children, students and teachers. These stories come from real events in actual schools in specific LEAs at particular times. They also come from all my own experiences - achievements, weaknesses, joys, fears . . . the lot! Within that paradigm of narrative research is the fact that we are 'licensed' – in life and in research – to tell some stories but not others. Some stories are too difficult to tell or hear and so are 'censored' in one way or another. The particular implications of this for me lie in the work that I do around the use of narrative in the reporting of research, for the accepted institutional form of academic research denies the truth of life narratives, and requires such truths to be subverted by the so-called objective/analytic which is little to do with how people really are – because passion is outlawed.

## Pieces I'd still own . . .

It can be argued that if curriculum is placed at the centre of special needs inquiry, then special needs provision will necessarily move nearer to the centre of curriculum issues, no longer marginalized but the very touchstone and proving point of coherent, sensitive and moral curriculum planning for all. Teaching and research on learning difficulties must move towards a curricular conception of special needs, and on the part of teacher and researcher alike this curricular approach will call for:

a. The framing of problems in the *whole* context in which they are noticed; such a frame will recognise the relevance of the aims and organisational structures of the *particular* institutions quite as much as the needs, motivations and intentions of all the individuals under study.
b. A theoretical framework which is capable of taking account of such complex interrelations by drawing on a *variety* of sociological, psychological and other theories rather than exclusively relying on any one of them.
c. A systematic recognition of the *experience* of participants – teachers, pupils and parents – in order better to understand and interpret teaching and research situations.
d. The empirical monitoring and documentation of learning events by both teachers and researchers leading to critical self-evaluation and appropriate revision of methodologies.

(1989, p. 337)

We are a long way from realising that research in the social sciences will only find in its theatres of inquiry what it put there. And this is particularly true of the field of SEN, whose origins in the measurement of behaviours endure as stark functions of policy.

For 'special education' is pre-eminently a world of paid-up meanings and attributions; in experience it issues from, and is set about with, meanings which are always readily to hand. This may be . . . to say no more than that the concept and, what is more, the experience of difference lie deep at the heart of the SEN discourse.

And as researchers of SEN or disability, we give shape and weight to these dimensions of difference: we do not come innocent to a task or a situation of events; rather we wilfully situate those events not merely in the institutional meanings which our profession provides but also, and in the same moment, we constitute them as expressions of our selves. Inevitably, the traces of our own psychic and social history drive us.

(1996, p. 138)

As researchers we need to ask ourselves the following critical questions:

• What responsibilities arise from the privileges I have as a result of my social position?
• How can I use my knowledge and skills to challenge, for example, the forms of oppression ... people experience?
• Does my writing and speaking reproduce a system of domination or [does it] challenge that system?'

(1996, p.144)

Listening to subjects with special educational needs throws into a particular relief all the generically difficult issues of researching 'voice' – issues to do with *who* is listening to *whom* and – above all, perhaps – *in whose interests*?

For the most part, life stories are articulated by the conventionally articulate . . . [some of whom] act politically through 'storied' voice specifically to emancipate; who ultimately seek, that is, a redistribution of power. Thus the search is for the articulation of a persuasive voice which will challenge readers' interests, privileges and prejudices.

As bell hooks has it, such writers can provide searing, harrowing 'chronicles of pain' – though she reminds us that these may well serve to 'keep in place existing structures of domination' if they do not bring about a deep unease in the reader.

How should we bring unease about?'

(1998, pp. 129–30)

When Rob Joynson was 43 years old, he came into school on a Tuesday morning much as usual, and passing at 10.40 by a maths class taken by Michelle G. – a probationer of 23 – and hearing terrible noise, and seeing through the window a boy at the back fetch a fat gob on Michelle's back as she walked down the aisle smiling, smiling, too, too nervously, her hands doing 'down, please; down, down' at the noise; and seeing this marbled yellow gob on Michelle's ordinary blouse on her decent body, Rob rushed into the room and to the back and took the boy – Mark something - by the ears, both ears, and pulled him up out of – through almost – his desk and repeatedly smashed his head against a chart of tessellations on the wall. And Michelle pulled at him from behind and screamed, and he twisted the boy down by his ears and pushed at him with his foot, kicking until the boy was quite under the desk. Then Rob started to cry and there was terrible silence – where there had been terrible noise – but for Rob searching for breath to fuel the small fearful wails that broke from him. When – thank god – someone laughed finally, unable to stay with the pain a moment longer, Rob fled the room.

(1999, pp. 429–30)

*The Story of Rob* . . . as a form of enquiry is identical with Michel Butor's project for the novel. In this respect, such a story may stand as all of a form, a metaphor and a model of research. As a form, its wholly linguistic character suggests its moral commitment to the reader's experience, without which its life is limited; as a metaphor for research it chiefly emphasises the urge to present veracious narrative; as a model it combines these virtues to show how the definition of reality is essentially a linguistic and therefore co-operative activity, directed at objects which it can never exhaust. But it is mainly as a form that it is valuable because given *with* its form is the obligation to search for form, failing which it can have nothing to say. The *Story of Rob* represents one such search for a form which will say educational difficulty.

(1999, p. 447)

# Profile

## *Jenny Corbett*
### *University of London Institute of Education, UK*

### Sample texts

*A Struggle for Choice: Students with Special Needs in Transition to Adulthood* (Corbett and Barton, 1992)

*Bad-Mouthing: The Language of Special Needs* (1996)

*Special Educational Needs in the Twentieth Century: A Cultural Analysis* (1998)

### Major influences

I have been involved in special education since I became fascinated by the needs of autistic children when I was studying as a trainee teacher in the mid-1960s. Looking more broadly than my higher education experience, I became concerned with the needs of disabled children from my own early childhood, as my father was a paediatrician and we used to visit the hospitals he worked in and to listen to his experiences and reflections. I got used to the idea that some children died young because of their disabilities and became well aware of the fact that doctors often did not know how to treat them. For example, I remember visiting hospitals in Hull in the 1950s where some children were lying in bed because their heads were so huge with hydrocephalus which doctors did not know how to treat. I remember that we took a boy with muscular dystrophy on an outing to Ilkley Moor and that he died soon afterwards in his early teens. My father was certainly a major influence on my attitude to special needs. We have something of a "love/hate" relationship, with me as the eldest of his four children. I enormously admire his professional integrity (he would only do National Health Service work, for example) but find him to be very inflexible. I suspect he found his very aggressive teenage daughter difficult to relate to and has been somewhat uneasy with me ever since, not being certain when I might 'blow up'! Yet, he has always been proud of my achievements, pressing me ever onwards whether I like it or not. I suspect my discomfort with the medical model of special needs is formed partly on ideological grounds but, also, partly because I have always felt the compulsion to challenge my father, who was a representative of the medical profession. We wrote a paper together in the early 1990s which was a very valuable way of sharing our perceptions on the development of the National Health Service and the way in which childhood disabilities have changed with new forms of medical intervention.

## Quotations from sample texts

The approach we are advocating, and through which we address the issues raised in this book, has the following features:

1 It is based on a belief that the manner in which a society deals with minority/disadvantaged groups provides some crucial insights into the nature of that society.
2 It locates the problems as not being within individuals but as arising from the discriminating practices and organisations of society.
3 It places the concern for integration within the wider perspective of human rights, social justice and equality of opportunity.
4 It advocates the importance of relational thinking and views critical analysis as an essential precondition for change.
5 It clarifies the nature of the opposition and the extent of the struggle involved if the changes demanded are to be realised.
6 It provides an antidote to the pursuit of slick, easy and short-term solutions for what are complex and fundamental issues.

(1992, p. 21)

Changing the way we use 'special needs' languages; conceptualizing fresh metaphors for disability; bringing marginalized discourses into the centre; reframing ways of listening; fostering unheard debates; relocating old hierarchies; forging new words in multiple arenas: all of this amounts to a frightening, wonderful potential for growth.

(1996, p. 35)

If new special languages are to form their own dominant discourses, representing and reflecting the various elements of disability culture, this will offer a cultural narrative with which the recipients of professional language can identify and use to redefine the terms of reference. This requires that status is given to the language of marginalized groups and that their metaphors are respected. Their ways of seeing will be different from the professionals and it will be easy to dismiss them as inaccurate and unreal. In the struggle with psychiatric diagnosis, this denial of unfamiliar narratives has long been a contentious issue. The fight to have cultural narratives validated is inextricably bound up with the social model of disability, civil rights and the personal as political.

(1996, p. 79)

I want to set special educational needs into a wider context in three key areas:
*historically*, to look back over the last century in order that the present and potential future can be better understood;
*internationally*, so that other cultures can be explored and their ways of responding to disability understood;
*at a community level*, by placing the experience of schooling into a deeper community context which includes issues of equity and entitlement, social roles and the valuing of individual and collective differences.

(1998, p. 1)

Entitlement is a concept which can only be measured in relation to what is available and what is perceived as a right in that context. Where the general population overall is given limited choices, it is not surprising that this will also be relevant for children with special educational needs. To apply Maslow's theory of value hierarchies, until basic needs are addressed it is difficult to prioritize individual aspects of emotional, aesthetic and spiritual well-being. My observation is that different societies choose different labels for special needs and use these labels in ways which reflect their cultural values. Countries like the USA, Australia and Britain have created an individualized culture in which self-awareness, self-fulfilment and self-help are concepts to be treated with respect and even reverence. It might be postulated that worship of self has taken the place of the church among many people in these cultures as a new and flourishing religion. This value system has major implications for the labelling of special needs. Rather than applying the broad, generic categories used by many poorer economies, these self-focused countries have created new labels and used these labels to demonstrate entitlement to resources.

(1998, p. 42)

## Reflections on inclusive education

I was a learning support co-ordinator in a further education college in the early 1980s which gave me real insight into the challenges, frustrations and rewards of inclusive education. The college prided itself on taking a high proportion of students in wheelchairs yet it was ill-prepared to accommodate the diverse learning styles of the students who were coming in from special schools. Those of us who were involved in trying to support the students and ensure that they had appropriate courses to attend were well aware that they still retained a marginalized status within the institution. They often felt socially isolated and some failed in the courses they attended because the work was inappropriate for them. While I was struggling at the grass roots to cope as best I could in frustrating circumstances, I was getting criticism from special needs advisers from the LEA. They came in to tell me that I was not encouraging sufficient inclusion as I allowed the disabled students, if they so requested, to stay in their own base room at lunch time rather than have to mix with their peers in the canteen.

It amuses me now that I am seen by some colleagues as a rabid inclusionist, when I was clearly seen as rather conservative in my practices then.

That experience made me very aware of the difficulties of delivering effective inclusive education. I felt then as I do now that, at an ideological level, it is the right way to go as a society and that learners should have the choice of going into mainstream provision. However, I am fully conscious of the challenges it presents. In my most recent research I am trying to find out more about the actual detail of pedagogy which effectively supports inclusive education. I am trying to learn from schools which feel they are effectively inclusive and have been developing their strategies for a number of years.

I suppose my own direct practitioner experience in the early 1980s reflects the early stages of inclusive education, where curriculum and pedagogy were rarely fully confronted. It is exciting for me now to be looking at examples of schools which have been working towards being effectively inclusive for over ten years. Pedagogy seems to me to be centrally important now. It is crucial to find ways of demonstrating that the learners who are included and those they are working with are all able to benefit and progress within the same learning environment. With the current emphasis on achievement, we need to examine that pedagogy which is both effectively inclusive and which values achievement.

## Links with different theoretical models

Most of those academics working in the special education area seem to have come through either a psychology or sociology route. My academic background has been in the humanities, specifically English literature. This has made me extremely interested in the use of language, metaphors and imagery. I suppose that *Bad-Mouthing* was my way of taking ownership of what I felt could be my own contribution to the special education debates. Writing style is important to me. I like writers who express their ideas clearly and I try to emulate them. My observations have been that it takes real skill to convey complex ideas in a simple, direct way. I think communication is vital. Students need to understand what we are trying to say to them. That is why we need to take care with the words we use.

Words are very important to me. That old saying, 'Sticks and stones will break your bones but words will never harm you', is complete rubbish in my mind. I have met so many adults who remember vividly when they were called 'Stupid' by their teacher in front of the class and how it made them feel then and often continue to feel. That is one of the reasons why

I am concerned about the words and labels we put on children. I think inclusive education, above all else, is about fostering a learning community which treats individuals with dignity and respect and it is about celebrating difference.

In recent years, I have become linked to disability studies especially in the way in which I have found similarities between gay pride and disability pride. My emphasis tends to be more upon the 'personal as political' rather than the social barriers alone. In my fifties I can now reflect that my own teenage feelings of invisibility and vulnerability, because I did not know what to do about my sexuality, influenced the way I went in my career. I think, at a subconscious level, I wanted to support vulnerable people because I felt so vulnerable myself. It may not have been the best of motivations, but I suspect I am not the only one who has sought comfort from special education. I think my current ability to be open about my sexuality has changed the way I am able to write. I am happy to include myself in my writing about special education, although I am very wary of becoming merely self-indulgent. I suppose I feel there needs to be a balance, in which we are not afraid to reveal our own subjective views and experiences as authors but in which we are also trying to find generalizable points which have broad implications. I do feel passionate about discrimination and the oppression of minorities, and this is bound to influence the way I write.

# Profile

## Mairian Corker
### University of Central Lancashire, UK

### Sample Texts

*Deaf and Disabled, or Deafness Disabled?* (1998)

*Disability Discourse* (Corker and French, 1999)

### Major influences

I came to disability in three ways. First I was born with an impairment (deafness), second I acquired physical disfigurement as a result of extensive surgery when I was a child, and third, I spent my adolescent years watching my clever and articulate father die from a brain tumour. In many ways these three 'facts' of my early life have brought disability into sharp relief in the here and now. Deafness is a huge issue in an academic culture based on communication, but the linguistic oppression I experienced at school – being teased in the showers, for example – was a result of my disfigurement and my 'lack' of knowledge of ordinary things – the things that other children knew. This could be compared with the experience of being in hospital for six months, where I received appropriate and extensive 'care,' and the regular, and largely inappropriate bodily invasion of audiologists, speech therapists and psychologists. My father's situation taught me about how cruel life is. In the eyes of his friends, post-diagnosis, he no longer existed, and it took away all the dignity he had left.

These experiences made me angry, and that anger made me into a rebel. Fortunately I went to a mainstream girls' school that encouraged us to be young feminists (before our time) and to think for ourselves. Learning gave me a creative channel for anger. Social justice is therefore something that drives me. It's a very strong motivator. I can't bear to see unfairness, and I am driven to speak out. Silence is the voice of complicity. So I've

74

never been able to be silent, and that's often a risky disposition to have.

Being in the mainstream system in the late 1950s and through the 1960s – and the socialist in me hates to admit that it was a private school – I received no 'specialist' intervention. Learning was my responsibility, and interestingly, that's how I still see it, but it was up to my teachers to nurture it. I think that my experience of school educationally was a very positive one – indeed, that school still has a very good rating in the league tables – but it wasn't typical. The learning environment was very liberal – or was it radical? Once I learnt what I was good at, I was allowed to pursue it even if it meant timetabling problems. That way it was more difficult to fail, but I had worked that out for myself. I'm particularly proud of my 'A' grade in English literature at 'A' level. But it's an irony that two of my fellow students (hearing) received prizes in English for their 'A' grades, while I got a prize for 'perseverence'.

But my social experience of school was soul-destroying. I had no friends other than a few teachers, with whom I developed very deep emotional attachments. I wasn't interested in boys (though I tried to be because it was expected) and that made me the butt of jokes (most of which I couldn't hear, but I saw the demeanour of those who delivered them). I didn't realize – Section 28 proponents take note – that this was all part of homophobic bullying, but then at the time, I didn't know there was a social category of people called lesbians because deaf students were only given 'necessary' information. I think that all of those experiences together certainly had to have an impact on me, particularly when I began to think about education in terms of oppression and what it means to be civilized.

In the 1980s I worked as an education officer with a major charity, the National Deaf Children's Society, where I had two main responsibilities. One was to try and keep abreast of what was happening 'on the ground' by visiting schools of all kinds. The second part of it was to be a parent advocate, which meant doing a lot of counselling and guidance work with parents, in addition to supporting them at LEA tribunals. To do this 'objectively' (whatever that means) I had to convince myself that I was working in the child's best interests when, in nine cases out of ten, it was about the parent's interests – in other words, they couldn't cope. That being said, the most sickening thing was the way in which LEA officials, who knew nothing at all about deafness or disability, were prepared to gamble these children's futures away in the interests of policy and resource availability.

Those deaf children remain in my mind constantly. I've been conscious for years of a forced schism between children's needs and government's, parent's and teachers' wants. Education as a whole is not really related to children's lives – to their insatiable curiosity and creativity – it just sees them as future capital who will 'fit' the system.

## Quotations from sample texts

Social model theorists often refer to the social creation of disability, whereas a poststructuralist would use the term social construction. But the difference between the meanings of the two terms is negligible, and so preference for one term over the other can say more about where social model theorists position themselves in relation to poststructuralist discourses.

However, the fact that we apparently use the same language does not mean that we share the same meaning. This can be explained by looking at deaf people's use of the deceptively simple term 'discussion'. Hearing people 'discuss' different topics often without thinking about it, and so do many deaf people – when they are with each other. But the minute the suggestion is made that I, as a deaf person, 'discuss' things with hearing people, I begin to ask questions about access, understanding, translatability, first and second languages and so on. So in these terms the meaning of 'discussion' has many added dimensions for me. If a hearing person imposes their meaning on me through social action after I have clarified that we do not mean the same thing by 'discussion', I may feel that I am being treated less favourably in the 'discussion', and because the hearing person's meaning is legitimated in the phonocentric culture, I may also feel disempowered and excluded – less able to contribute to the 'discussion'. The problem can be resolved by 'discussion' – or can it?

(1998, pp. 59–60)

The issue of linguistic and cultural differences is clearly a significant one which disabled people are already addressing, but it goes well beyond the 'nice' words and the 'nasty' words relating to disability that are in cultural circulation. Indeed, to view language only in these terms is to take a monologic view of discourse, when even within monologues meaning is contextualized in different ways which interact with each other. Even if we were to find consistent language which was acceptable to all disabled people, we would still not fully account for the different ways that language operates within discursive practice, and it is here that language is critically linked to issues of knowledge, and ultimately power, because particular forms of knowledge are privileged.

(1999, pp. 192–3)

## Reflections on inclusive education

I was responsible for responding to the first round of National Curriculum consultation documents for the NDCS (National Deaf Children's Society). I am conscious that I was trying to write from the children's perspectives, particularly as I had just done some research on young deaf children's views on 'integration'. On the basis of responses from other organizations for disabled children, it was clear that everyone had very deep concerns, and most thought that though the ideology seemed OK, the pragmatics were rubbish – 'We are having a curriculum for all', a utopian theory, but nothing about how that was going to be achieved. We felt these proposals were a step backwards for political reasons. Predictably, our views were ignored and I became convinced at that point that politicians don't live in the real world and have no idea about the enormous variety of ways in which children learn.

Recently, through doing ethnographic research with disabled children, I've become even more convinced that we still have to get to grips with this thing called 'inclusion' on a philosophical level much more clearly before we can even begin with the practice. What, for example, is the logic behind saying, on the one hand, that you want inclusive education and on the other, specifying that this is to be achieved through segregated policy, staff and, sometimes, curriculum? What is the point in including disabled children in a system that excludes or marginalizes disability knowledge *per se* from a learning point of view? Why does government never ask 'Inclusion into what?' Why do disabled children more often get placed in schools with poor academic records? Why do disabled children from special schools experience culture shock when they move to college or university? These are the most important questions.

I don't think government really has a vision of a civil society. What is it to be a good citizen in *contemporary* society? What is it to have rights? What is it to have responsibilities? I don't think we can understand or practice inclusion unless all of these things are related to children's lives in the here and now, and not in terms of future capital or past values.

I don't like using the term 'special needs' – it's paradoxical to 'inclusion'. I worry that it is increasingly part of a labelling process that is used to pick children off or as a justification for a lack of or a redistribution of resources in a way that is not in the child's interests. These labels are very dehumanizing – they really get to the nub of why we are disabled people and not people with disabilities. Whatever the level of education, what seems to be important is to assess the physical and social environment to see what has to be changed to ensure that it is conducive to inclusion. I think we also need to be developing teachers who like and respect children and are prepared to encourage their knowledge and creativity, not teachers who are 'experts' on deafness or blindness or learning difficulty. I think for many kids, and most especially for disabled kids, education's not stimulating or exciting any more – it's a process of being offered a script and told to learn it. The Internet might help encourage creativity, but I imagine it won't be long before the government tells schools which web-sites the children can log into and which they can't.

## Links with different theoretical models

Like many in disability studies, I continue to be hugely influenced by the scholarship and political energy of people like Mike Oliver and Vic Finkelstein. But I've also become critical of the neo-Marxist, sociological orientation of their work, which is something I hope they would encourage as academics and activists! It remains of vital importance for me that they are disabled academics as this puts a stamp of credibility on their work. This critique doesn't, I think, identify me as a neo-liberal, but it does very much reflect my position as a feminist social theorist as opposed to a sociological theorist. Social theory is, by its very nature, inter-disciplinary and so I am also influenced by ideas from applied linguistics, anthropology and the new sociology of childhood, for example. I get frustrated with disciplinary boundaries.

All of these areas are, to some extent, looking at both the formal and informal contexts in which people learn – at both individual agency and social structure – because really learning, communication and identity are somewhere between the two. Informal, local interaction seems important to me. I'd like to think that it is in this area that my contribution to the field is located. As a writer, however, I've become used to the 'writer's vacuum' that means that the impact of what I write is largely invisible unless I actively pursue feedback. If I had the choice, I would rather be visible *only* through my text and encourage people to read what I write carefully and critically (by which I mean critique, not criticism). That's one way that I try to get away from ideas about authority, because I'm not comfortable with monoliths, especially the monolith of special education, and in that I'm very influenced in different ways by the theoretical work of Judith Butler, Dorothy Smith and Mikhail Bakhtin.

I do think it's important and healthy for any field to have dissenting voices, and the way the field deals with these is a measure of its commitment to growth. The key for me is to dialogue not to damn! So really, I see myself in the role of the questioner – the one who says 'But . . .' – not for the sake of it, but because I know that a lot of people, many disabled children among them, are frightened to say this, or think 'What's the point . . . they won't listen anyway'. Disability theory is very adult- and macro-focused, and as such it can't be of much help in local, micro-analysis of children's agency. With disabled children, we forget about the informal part of their lives, but I suspect that this is where most of their learning, both positive and negative, takes place. I have found the work of Ray McDermott, and Étienne Wenger's work on 'communities of practice' useful in the area of informal learning.

On teaching practice I am interested by theories about reflexivity. Teachers rarely get to see how they interact with the children, or to see the children's verbal and non-verbal reactions to them when they are teaching because everything happens so fast in the classroom. The result is that par-ticular social practices become very deeply embedded in the process of education and in teachers' minds. I think teachers need to have the oppor-tunity to get constructive, helpful feedback (and to be 'beaten up' occa-sionally!) on how they behave towards children while they are teaching. There are ways that disabled children and adults can contribute to an ongoing process of training if the profession would only open itself to it.

For me, that kind of approach would be far more helpful than the current inspection process, which seems to demoralize people more than anything. I have watched inspectors at work and have thought 'How can you possibly understand what is going on here when you come in for one week, often sit at the back of the room and rely on what's verbalized, don't get involved, and don't talk to the children away from the watchful eye of adults? How can you know if this is good practice when you don't have very high expectations?' I don't think this is a worst case scenario. I've seen 'special needs' provision being 'commended' when the children seem to be part of no visible learning process.

In FE accreditation is a proxy for quality and, so far, no one has been able to come up with a way to validate informal or unstructured learning activity. The explanation we are given is 'that students only go to college to pass exams', but the reality, I suspect is that informal learning is not valued because it can't be assessed in concrete ways. Validating one kind of learning creates a two-tier structure, but it particularly impacts on disabled students who have already been disadvantaged by the same system in compulsory education. That's really the only sense of progression they get – the disadvantage I mean. All of this seems to be part of the commercialization of the public sector and I don't like it.

Changes in theory have often been as cosmetic as changes in language. For example, the change in language from using the term 'integration' to using the term 'inclusion' doesn't mean anything has changed underneath that. In deaf education, which we always have to view as separate for some reason, there may be more sign language but there isn't a parallel concept of what that means for inclusion. There also seems to me to be a very simplistic and limited understanding of the relationship between cognitive skills and language skills. When I see deaf children struggling in education, it's often because they haven't got experientially relevant concepts to describe, not because they haven't got the language to describe them. On the other hand I think deaf kids 'know' rather more than adults assume, but they aren't given credit for it because 'deaf' knowledge is devalued. The moves towards sign language are positive, particularly from the social perspective, but the provision of sign is still patchy and inconsistent, and in many schools the children can sign better than the teachers *because* they interact informally with each other and because they're deaf.

Changing the language is not the whole answer, and especially not when it become associated with some kind of fixed identity that children are moulded into. In my mind, it's arguable whether this is any better than talking about 'disabled children' as some kind of objective category. What really resonates with me, and what disabled children have consistently emphasized, is the view that inarticulateness is not a disability, but an invitation to listen in a new way.

# Reflection

## Harry Daniels
*University of Birmingham, UK*

### Sample texts

Visual displays as tacit relays of the structure of pedagogic practice (1989)

*Charting the Agenda: Educational Activity after Vygotsky* (1993)

Pedagogic practices, tacit knowledge and discursive discrimination: Bernstein and post-Vygotskian research (1995)

*Secondary School Mathematics and Special Educational Needs* (Daniels and Anghileri, 1995)

*An Introduction to Vygotsky* (1996a)

Back to basics: three 'r's for special needs education (1996b)

An intercultural comparative study of the relation between different models of pedagogic practice and constructs of deviance (Daniels *et al.*, 1996)

*Teacher Support Teams in Primary and Secondary Schools* (Creese, Daniels and Norwich, 1997)

*How to Set Up and Develop a Teacher Support Team* (Parrilla and Daniels, 1998)

*Emotional and Behavioural Difficulty in Mainstream Schools* (Daniels, Visser and Cole, 1999)

Issues of equity in special needs education as seen from the perspective of gender (Daniels *et al.*, 1999)

*Inclusive Education: World Yearbook of Education 1999* (Daniels and Garner, 1999)

I started my academic career as a geneticist working in the field of plant breeding. One of the major theoretical questions of the day was referred to as the problem of genotype–environment interaction. The concern here was with the extent to which the same seed would flourish differentially in different contexts. Mathematical models were built in which main-factor effects were attributed to the genotype, the environment, and, in an error term, the interaction between the two. Even in plants this was not entirely satisfactory. Years later, when the deputy head teacher of a special school, I had the opportunity of visiting a number of special schools (moderate learning difficulty) maintained by the same local education authority. The variation in organization management and pedagogy to be found in these schools was remarkable. It led me to consider whether a referral to such a school could possibly have any kind of uniform effect on pupils. I became concerned about the relationship between how children think and feel and the social and cultural organization of the institution in which they were placed.

My previous post in education had been in an authority which referred very few pupils to special needs provision. My then current LEA maintained a very high level of special provision. This transition between one administrative culture and another caused me to reflect on the social construction of criteria for inclusion and exclusion in that which counted as the mainstream. At the time I was studying for a diploma which placed considerable emphasis on psychological accounts of children's difficulty in learning. It seemed to me that this was necessary but not sufficient for explaining children's experiences of schooling. What I was looking for was a theoretical account which would relate social and cultural circumstances to individual functioning.

I found the writing of the Russian L. S. Vygotsky to be a useful starting point in trying to understand how schools as institutions created demands which both shaped the performance of individuals and yet were also influenced by them. I explored this body of theory in Daniels (1993; 1996a).

Much of the work which I was reading had cited speech as the primary mediator between the social and the individual. It had also tended to speak only of cognitive factors rather than affective matters. In Daniels (1989) I attempted to understand a little more about the ways in which the visual environments of schools acted as information relays concerning the social, cultural and pedagogic priorities in which pupils were placed. Here then I was seeking to extend the analysis of semiotic mediation beyond speech. In Daniels (1995) I returned to the study of speech itself but with particular emphasis on the subject specific nature of speech as required in a particular curriculum configuration. The policy implication of this work is that if we seek to prepare children for 'reintegration' into particular forms of institutional life then we have to consider the forms of special schooling in terms of the patterns of communicative competence which they privilege.

In Daniels *et al.* (1996) we took the analysis of cultural effects a stage further. Our concern was with the school specific definitions of deviance which arose in specific forms of pedagogic practice in two countries – Denmark and England. We showed that the institutional effect was probably more powerful that the state effect in the case of these two countries. Irrespective of the state background, differences in school culture gave rise to significant differences in pupil and teacher definitions of deviance.

Taken together these three papers argue that the structure of school organization, in fact the sociocultural historical nature of schools generates messages and possibilities for pupil position which must surely be important in the analysis of who is accepted and who is not accepted within them. In Daniels and Anghileri (1995) we sought to apply some of these understandings to the case of secondary school mathematics. Our ongoing work on gender (see Daniels *et al.*, 1999) brings the post Vygotskian sociocultural view into play with poststructuralist views on masculinity and femininity in order to understand matters of gender issues in learning in schools.

In much of our work on EBD (emotional and behavioural difficulty) (Daniels, Visser and Cole, 1999) we have shown that patterns of staff relation and forms of pedagogic discourse in schools have a significant effect on the possibilities for widening participation in mainstream schooling. We argue that collaborative patterns of staff working and the retention of a discourse of values in education within a school are key indicators in what we define as good practice. The creation and development of collaborative problem-solving groups in schools in England (Creese, Daniels and Norwich, 1997) and Spain (Parrilla and Daniels, 1998) followed the argument that collaborative social environments enhance the cognitive potential of institutions.

I would thus argue that we need to pursue research themes that explore intra- and inter-systemic relations (see Figure 2.1).

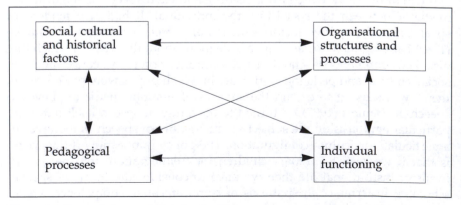

**Figure 2.1** Research for special needs education

We need to understand ways in which social, cultural and historical contexts condition our values and beliefs particularly with respect to organization and pedagogy.

For example we need:

- to understand and to be able to change the values and beliefs associated with intelligence and effort as they impact on teaching and learning in different cultural contexts.
- to understand and be able to change the ways in which assumptions about masculinity impacts on pedagogic practice and are made manifest in management practices. (I would also add that we need to understand the way that notions of masculinity are socially acquired and evaluate their impact on learning.

We also need to understand much more about the way in which social and cultural products condition and transform learning (see Daniels and Garner, 1999). The psychological tools and signs that mediate pedagogic relationships vary as a function of cultural, historical and importantly institutional context. In addition people with disabilities may experience limited access to specific means of mediation, e.g. speech in the case of hearing impairment. We need to know much more about the relationship between socially available and personally accessible tools and signs and cognitive development.

We need to understand much about relationships between organizational structures and processes, pedagogical processes and individual functioning. Crucially we need to try and find ways of supporting the development of responsive pedagogic and institutional practices (Daniels, 1996b).

# Profile

## *Alan Dyson*
### *University of Newcastle, UK*

### Sample texts

It's not what you do – it's the way that you do it: setting up a
  curriculum for less-able high school pupils (1981)

Social and educational disadvantage: reconnecting special needs
  education (1997)

*New Directions in Special Needs: Innovations in Mainstream Schools*
  (Clark *et al.*, 1997)

### Major influences

Among the influences on my work, the most important, undoubtedly, is
the impact of being born into a working-class family in Yorkshire a few
years after the end of the Second World War. The memory I have is not
one so much of economic poverty, but of poverty of opportunity. My
parents, along with most of their generation, had been denied any but the
most basic education and, as a result, were trapped in an endless cycle of
manual work. They tried many times to find escape routes, but the idea
that anyone can forge a better life for themselves simply through hard
work and enterprise is, as their experience attests, a nonsense.

The fact, therefore, that I had much greater educational opportunities –
first as a 'grammar school boy' and then as a student at what in the late
1960s was a 'new' university – has left me with an unshakeable faith
(however misplaced) in education as a crucial generator of opportunities
for otherwise disadvantaged children.

That faith was more than a little tested, I admit, by my first experiences
of teaching in an inner-city comprehensive school. Suffice it to say that my

skills in riot control improved as my first year in teaching went on. The scars that remained, however, still give me a keen sense of the difficulties which teachers in such schools face, day by day, minute by minute. At the same time, the experience also convinced me that an education system which alienated and then discarded so many children and young people was massively unjust. Their humanity, already compromised by the circumstances into which they were born was, in some cases, damaged beyond repair by the inflexibility, the elitism and the 'institutional carelessness' which I saw all around me and which outweighed the best efforts of even the most well-intentioned teachers.

I also acquired both from my own upbringing and from that first experience an abiding concern with the education of those 'failures' in and of the system. I work now in the field of special needs education because, at that time, it was the most obvious mechanism for making at least a token attempt to redress the disadvantages which such children experienced. For 13 years as a teacher, therefore, and throughout my academic career, I sought better ways of engaging such students in learning and opening up to them some equivalent of the sorts of opportunities which I myself have had. In particular, because I have tended to see the problem as structural, I have (rightly or wrongly) also tended to seek structural solutions – in terms, at least, of organization and policy rather than of classroom practice.

My early inspirations (for such they were) were not so much individual commentators or whole pieces of work, but ideas and phrases that seemed to capture some exciting new way of seeing things – I think in particular of Golby and Gulliver's (1979) critique of remedial education as the 'ambulance service' of an accident-prone education system, of Tony Booth's (1983) definition of special needs as 'those needs to which schools currently do not respond' (the only definition anyone need bother with), and of my one-time headteacher, Ian Galletley's (1976) exhortation that remedial departments should 'do away with' themselves. Add to these snippets from Herbert Kohl (1973) and Paulo Freire (1972) and you have a pantheon of radical influences that made me one of the most dangerously shambolic teachers ever to stalk the corridors of a comprehensive school!

My own first attempts at writing up my work betrayed these influences (Dyson, 1981; 1985; 1990a; 1990b). However, I also learnt from bitter experience that schools did not change easily through the efforts of the sort of 'hero-innovator' that I aspired to be. This sense that schools and education systems are even more difficult to work with than alienated children continues to make me less sanguine, I suspect, than many other commentators in this field. In particular, it makes me far from convinced that special needs education, even in some reconstructed form, provides anything like an adequate platform from which to bring about the sorts of educational changes which I believe to be necessary. The concern of much of my later work, therefore, has been to try to understand what the idealistic principles with which I started might mean in the midst of the hard realities of challenging students, intractable educational organizations and systems and, above all, the patterns of structural inequality within which all attempts at change are located. Indeed, I mistrust deeply, any attempt at idealism which fails to take such realities into account.

## Quotations from sample texts

For many years now, voices have been raised warning how the nature of our schools created a group which was by definition 'subnormal', or 'backward'. . . And yet we still get demands from the most authoritative sources for a curriculum which will be fixed and unchanging, the same for all children. What has become increasingly obvious to me is this: if the curriculum is a static entity, formulated without reference to specific children, it will inevitably create a group of children for whom it is, for whatever reason, unsuitable; it will require those children to be called 'stupid'; and it will call into being remedial departments to do something, if not about the stupidity itself, then at least about its most obvious manifestations. If remedial departments in secondary schools are not to be simply the hammers for knocking the pupil square pegs into the round holes of the traditional academic disciplines, they have to become actively involved in breaking down the static curriculum. They have to look at how decisions about their children are made in the school at least as much as at what those decisions are. And they have to find some way from their position at the bottom of the hierarchy in which they can cause those decisions to take into account not just some fixed view of what knowledge is but the wishes of the children, the interests of their teachers, and some global view of the needs and nature of each individual child.

(1981, pp. 122–3)

Special needs education has, over the past two and a half decades, gradually lost such grip as it may once have had on the relationship between children's difficulties in school and wider patterns of socio-economic disadvantage and inequality . . . I am increasingly convinced that special needs education, as we currently have it, is incapable of addressing certain fundamental failings and inequities in our education system; much less within society as a whole. I wish to suggest, therefore, that we need a fundamental refocusing of our energies and our attention.

(1997, p. 155)

In recent years, there has been much concern with the question of whether it is possible to construct an approach to diversity which will take us 'beyond special needs' – a concern to which we admit to having contributed ourselves . . . As we have reviewed in the course of this book attempts to explore this question over the last two decades, we are forced to the inevitable conclusion that it is the wrong question to ask. Of course, it matters greatly whether our schools are capable of responding to diversity so that all children learn effectively. It also matters whether that response is made at the expense of the participation of all members of our society in the central social institution of the 'community' school offering a common set of experiences in shared classrooms. The question, therefore, of whether a whole school approach or an 'innovatory' approach, or 'inclusive education' or some other approach will achieve the optimum realization of these two imperatives is an important one.

However, in the final analysis the answer to that question depends crucially on the answers to far more fundamental questions – questions to do with what we believe education to be about, what we believe children should learn, what kind of society we wish to create and, ultimately, who the 'we' is who should debate and decide these things. These questions are complex and contentious – but they are the ones that all those involved in what we currently call 'special needs education' must now ask.

(Clark *et al.*, 1997, pp. 190–1)

## Reflections on inclusive education

For many, 'inclusion' seems to offer a new way forward. The biography which I have set out above, however, leaves me deeply ambivalent on this matter. I welcome the liberal and even radical intentions that are implied by the notion of inclusion. I applaud and support the aim of enabling all learners to be present in mainstream schools and of maximizing their participation in the lives of those schools once they are present.

However, I am not convinced that presence and participation are, of themselves, enough to address the deep structural inequalities which many children experience. It is as though all the efforts so far have focused on the critical and deconstructive step of removing the barriers that undoubtedly characterize the education system in its current form. Simply removing barriers, however, is unlikely to change to any significant degree, the life-chances of many children. If nothing else, new and more subtle barriers will simply emerge to take their place. What I would like to address, in the years of research and writing I have left, therefore, is the question of what sort of education should be on offer as we seek to bring those barriers down. Perhaps we do indeed want all children together in the same place, participating in the same experiences – but to do what, and to what end? These are questions, I suggest, that we have not even begun to ask.

# Profile

## *Lani Florian*
### *University of Central Lancashire, UK*

## Sample texts

Inclusive education in the marketplace (Rouse and Florian, 1997)

An examination of the practical problems associated with the implementation of inclusive education policies (1998)

Defining difference: a comparative perspective on legal and policy issues in education reform and special educational needs (Florian and Pullin, 2000)

## Major influences

Though it is not always easy for professionals like me to hear what disabled people have to say, the voices of disabled people describing their experience of disability in society exert a powerful influence on my thinking. Trying to understand disability from the perspective of a disabled person constantly challenges the way I think about my work as a researcher and, I would like to think, advocate. Resources like the publications from the Disabilities Studies Project at Hunter College in New York, and books like *Making Difficulties: Research and the Construction of Special Educational Needs*, edited by Peter Clough and Len Barton (1996), have helped to make it possible for professionals to hear these voices.

In addition, the students I taught over the years have been major influences on my thinking. As a newly qualified teacher, I had a job in an alternative school for 'delinquent' pupils. All of the students were on probation, and the school and halfway house where they lived was seen as a last chance before incarceration. As I got to know my students I began to realize that they were not 'pupils with special educational needs' but boys and girls without advocates. They had been in trouble in school or had been caught breaking social rules, i.e. shoplifting etc., but, unlike other people I knew, they had no one in their lives to help them sort it out. This experience made me realize our common humanity and I began to question the segregation of other groups of people as well.

Another powerful influence on my thinking at that time was a little book called *Anger and the Rocking Chair: Gestalt Awareness with Children*, written by a teacher, Janet Lederman. The book showed me how a teacher could work in a therapeutic way without compromising her teaching. Though the book is now dated and long out-of-print, I keep my copy as a powerful reminder of the vulnerability of pupils and the power of teachers as healers.

## Quotations from sample texts

Even within a supportive legislative framework, the implications of inclusion for schools are enormous, affecting such issues as: organization, teaching styles, curriculum, assessment, staff development and community links. In this paper, we argue that the task has been made greater because schools are operating in a hostile legislative context. During the past decade, there has been a shift from legislation and policies based upon principles of equity, social progress and altruism, to new legislation under-pinned by a market-place philosophy based on principles of academic excellence, choice and competition. In a climate in which educational reforms are based upon the principles of the market, students with disabilities and/or special educational needs are particularly vulnerable. For schools, the task of becoming inclusive is to swim against the tide of educational reform.

(1997, p. 324)

Despite the difficulties associated with the implementation of inclusive education policies, there is a great deal of philosophical agreement about the rights of children with special educational needs to equal educational opportunity. The concept of inclusion is a central theme in the new government's education policies. The extent to which the consultative process currently underway will help to ensure that pupils with special educational needs are justly included in the new education reform proposals is unclear. However, the acknowledgement of special educational need within a call for high standards which benefit all pupils is an exciting development, though, as the debate on the viability of inclusive education as a model for special education shows, there are many problems to overcome.

(1998, p. 108)

In the United States, recent efforts have reflected a desire for enhanced accountability for the performance of all students, including students with disabilities. At the same time, there is now an effort to move away from categorising and labelling students with disabilities, to a system of making federal support available for the proportions of students needing extra educational services. This increased recognition of responsibility for the performance of all students, coupled with a de-emphasis on the use of structured systems of labelling disabilities, suggest both a broader perspective on the necessity for successfully educating all students and a willingness to undertake new approaches to pursuing this goal . . . future education policies could be built around the possibility that what appears marginal (i.e. a disability or learning difficulty) is actually a fundamental aspect of the human condition, in that a disability or disabling condition can be acquired by anyone at any time. This kind of reorientation in thinking about disability could be applied in the areas of housing, transportation and employment policy.

An application of this reorientation of thinking about disability to education would require policies which acknowledge that the needs and abilities of all pupils are not static but constantly changing. Such an acknowledgement would permit the much-needed flexibility required for the building of human capital in a world where both the incidence and nature of disability are subject to change.

(2000, pp. 34–35)

## Reflections on inclusive education

As I reflect on inclusive education, I think it is easier said than done. The marginalization of particular groups of people, as immoral as it is, seems to serve some kind of protective function in society (e.g. 'We're OK because they are not'). This operates on many levels and is very difficult to overcome. Recent work linking the special needs task to school improvement, and research that attempts to isolate the conditions for inclusive practice, and teaching and learning are important steps forward. However, I don't think we have fully grasped the complexity of the task.

## Links with different theoretical models

Each of the different theoretical models (biological, psychodynamic, behavioural, ecological and social) contributes to our overall understanding of disability though they may lead to different implications for the practice of inclusive education. The theoretical emphasis and associated research paradigms of each model helps us to understand how different factors such as family, culture, schooling and biology can combine in different ways to produce 'disability' and/or result in the exclusion or marginalization of different people from the 'mainstream'. I think it is important to study the range of theoretical models and to understand the relative contribution of each to our thinking about disability, and to understand how they influence the work we do.

# Reflection: experiencing 'special' and 'normal' education

## Sally French
### Brunel University, UK

## Sample texts

Memories of school: 1958–1962 (1992)

'Can you see the rainbow?': the roots of denial (1993)

Equal opportunities . . . yes please! (1994)

Surviving the institution: working as a visually disabled lecturer in higher education (1998)

Many of my visually impaired friends were sent to residential special schools at the age of five. I avoided this fate as a tiny country primary school (with 30 pupils and threatened with closure) accepted me. It was not the local school and involved me in a walk of several miles every day. I managed well, and was never teased or bullied, but I often felt separate and different from the other children. One of the problems was that the adults did not understand my disability and tended not to believe me when I tried to explain:

> On warm, sunny days we had our lessons outdoors where, because of the strong sunlight, I could not see to read, write or draw. It was only when the two teachers realised I was having similar difficulties eating my dinner that they began to doubt their interpretation that I was a malingerer.
>
> (1993, p. 70)

Experiences such as this have given me a deep respect for the knowledge of children however young they may be.

At the age of nine it was decided that I should go to a special residential

91

school for partially sighted girls. I do not know how or why this decision was made though my parents had very little say. The school, where I remained for four years, was like something out of Dickens:

> When we arrived back at school, our stomachs churning with home-sickness, we would each be given two Lincoln biscuits and a cup of icy cold milk. No-one dared to cry. Then we would listen with great apprehension while list after list was read out concerning what table we would sit on for meals, what dormitory we would sleep in, who our walking partner on the long crocodile walks would be, and where we would do our housework each day. We all so badly wanted to be with friends but the lists were carefully devised to avoid this as far as possible.
>
> (1992, p. 45)

Yet despite this the experience had a deeply positive side:

> Attending special school at the age of nine was, in many ways, a great relief. Despite the crocodile walks, the bells, the long separations from home, the regimentation and the physical punishment, it was an enormous joy to be with other partially sighted children and to be in an environment where limited sight was simply not an issue. I discovered that lots of other children shared my world and, despite the harshness of institutional life, I felt relaxed, made lots of friends, became more confident and thrived socially. For the first time in my life I was a standard product and it felt very good.
>
> (1993, p. 71)

The educational standards were so poor in this school that I reached the top class by the age of twelve. I was then transferred to another residential school with a good academic reputation and a rather demanding ethos:

> The headmaster, a strong, resolute pioneer in the education of partially sighted children appeared to have a genuine belief not only that we were as good as everyone else but that we were almost certainly better . . . He liked us to regard ourselves as sighted and steered us away from any connection with blindness: for example, although we were free to go out by ourselves to the nearby town and beyond, the use of white canes was never suggested though many of us use them now. He delighted in people who broke new, visually challenging ground, like acceptance at art school and reading degrees in mathematics, and 'blind' occupations, like physiotherapy, were rarely encouraged. In many ways his attitudes and behaviour were refreshing, yet he placed the onus to achieve and succeed entirely on ourselves; there was never any suggestion that the world could adapt, or that our needs could or should be accommodated.
>
> (1993, p. 73)

So much time had been wasted in the first special school that I did not succeed and I left just before my 16th birthday with no qualifications expect Pitman's elementary typewriting. I worked for two years as an assistant housemother (in a residential school for physically disabled children) and in 1967 I gained a place at my local college of further education for a one year GCE O-level course:

The college had never taken a visually impaired student before but after much deliberation and anxious discussion they decided to accept me provided I could manage without any extra help or support. Despite their pronouncements that no one would assist me, many staff proved eager to help on an individual basis. The English teacher wrote all her comments with a thick, black pen so that I could read them, the biology teacher gave me duplicate diagrams of those she drew on the blackboard and the history teacher, whose enthusiasm for the subject would have made anyone's lack of access entirely intolerable to him, abandoned visual aids altogether . . . Not everyone was helpful but the modest assistance I was given there was greater than anything I have since received despite all the guidelines and policy documents that have been produced in the name of equal opportunities.

(1994, p. 155)

So after seven years of 'special' education I gained six O-levels on a crash course in a 'normal' college. This was sufficient (in those days) to commence physiotherapy training:

At the age of 19, after working for two years, I started my physiotherapy training at a special segregated college for blind and partially sighted students. For the first time in my life my disability was, at least in part, defined as blindness. Although about half the students were partially sighted, one of the criteria for entry to the college was the ability to read and write braille (which I had never used before) and to type proficiently as, regardless of the clarity of their handwriting, the partially sighted students were not permitted to write their essays or examinations by hand, and the blind students were not permitted to write theirs in braille. No visual teaching methods were used in the college and, for those of us with sight, it was no easy matter learning subjects like anatomy, physiology and biomechanics without the use of diagrams.

(1993, p. 75)

Although the student numbers in this college (run by the Royal National Institute for the Blind) were very low (there were just 13 in my year) no attempt was made to cater for our individual needs. This is justified in the following patronizing statement from the college literature:

No difference is made between students who are totally blind and those with some degree of residual vision. All training is based on totally blind techniques. This is essential as, even with a stable prognosis, provision must be made for eventual function as a blind person. It is also a fact that many partially sighted students think they can see more than they can; their accuracy is improved when they accept a 'blind' technique . . . a degree of vision should only be regarded as a bonus.

(North London School of Physiotherapy for the Visually Handicapped, 1981, p. 10)

Having other people decide how much I could and could not see felt like being a child again.

In 1978, after four years as a physiotherapist, I trained as a physiotherapy lecturer and have been a lecturer in higher education ever since. During this time I have gained four degrees through evening study in four separate universities. I can certainly think of individuals who were helpful but nowhere have my needs been met on anything more than a 'goodwill' level. This also applies to employment:

> Equal opportunity statements, good interview practice and quotas can very often lull disabled people into a false sense of security, rendering us less able to make an informed choice. This happened to me in a university that has a good reputation on the inclusion of disabled students. I discovered when in the post, however, that the organisation would not accommodate me. I found myself trying to read microscopic print and appalling handwriting or going to meetings when none of the information was in an accessible format for me. I could not see the numbers or names on the doors and found the layout of the campus confusing, a problem that was exacerbated by inaccessible signs. I found myself yearning for the 'bad old days' when, though dialogue was blunt ('you can work here provided you can manage like everyone else') we, as visually disabled individuals, knew exactly where we were!

(1998, p. 38)

I'm an academic and a perpetual student. It's what I want to be and it feels right for me, but I do it at considerable cost to myself.

# Reflection: 'There ain't no theory as far as I can see ...'

## Gillian Fulcher

### Freelance Educational Consultant, Australia

### Sample texts

*Disabling Policies? A Comparative Approach to Education Policy and Disability* (1989)

Schools and contests: A reframing of the effective schools debate? (1993)

A novel's view of the corporate fantasy (1998)

I began writing about integration and disabled students in 1983. I was seconded to assist a Ministerial Review of Educational Services for the Disabled. My task was to write a report on the committee's deliberations to provide policy for the Minister. As I took notes in the sometimes 12-hour meetings, and talked and watched what was going on in that very large committee, and fended off my opponents, and watched power being brokered in the bureaucracy – the Education Department of Victoria – all day, I wondered what this thing called policy was. A year later, back at the university, I thought the literature would tell me. It didn't. I wrote a book (1989) to work it out.

The main ideas in my writing is that policy is political: it is 'the outcome of political states of play in policy arenas' (Fulcher, 1989, p. 15). Integration is a political objective. Politics shift. The words change: inclusion, for instance, has overtaken integration. The tactics change, and the conditions under which people may act change, but the objectives of groups and individuals remain. I didn't fully digest these ideas when I wrote the book or I shouldn't have been able to write some of the first paragraph: the bit

95

that asks why some policies frequently fail.

The idea of a theory of a political objective I think is false. How can we have theories about political states of play? We can have theories about enduring aspects of our world, or types of society, or notions that solidarity is an important aspect of societies, or theories of the class structure, or of politics for instance. Theories of politics help us understand the politics surrounding integration but that isn't a theory of integration.

In writing policy on integration I brought to it an interest in the idea of equality – it was that, and my sociological background which got me the job. That interest probably predated my late university studies as a sociologist. Again, equality is a goal which I think can hardly be achieved but which, nevertheless, is worth striving for, for it can make some things more likely. But it has its dangers, as Orwell wrote, in *Animal Farm*. I brought too, a long-standing interest in justice and its opposite. I wrote about this in 'Schools and contests: a reframing of the effective schools debate?' (1994). It's a dense paper, packed with questions as I sought to widen my view of the conditions which might affect integration for some children in some places. Justice is a study in itself. It needs locating in theories of a society's political institutions. And in turn, those institutions require a theory of the wider society.

On the latter, I found Barry Hindess's work invaluable. I began with his short, almost too concise paper, 'Actors and social relations' (1986). His notion of the corporation as a social actor drew our attention, in ways which differed from earlier theories, about the rule by large corporations, and it anticipates by some years our acceptance in everyday speech of phrases such as the corporation as a good corporate citizen: these phrases are misleading. I read as much as I could of Hindess's work, acquiring his papers before they were published, pondering his elegant words and provocative ideas about the nature of democracy and politics. Any discussion of the political agenda of integration needs placing in this context: the broader institutions affect what is possible at lower levels, though, as Hindess asserts, they do not determine what is possible. Social life can be wonderfully surprising. That is why, despite the rules – of which there are now far too many on disability, a consequence of our striving to influence policy – the unexpected can be achieved. In some school, without the necessary help, some teacher may find room for a child someone else will say is too difficult or not 'appropriate'. That summary statement is misleading since it suggests teachers make decisions at their whim: this isn't at all the case, and the detail to back up the statement can be found in many places, and partly in my book, *Disabling Policies? A Comparative Approach to Education Policy and Disability*.

The major influences on my thinking about the sociology of disability were Len Barton and Sally Tomlinson in their early collections of papers, in 1984, for instance, and especially Tomlinson's (1982) *A Sociology of*

*Special Education.* As I grappled with the committee's deliberations, I told my research assistant to walk the streets until she found a copy. I still remember Marion's face as she brought it back. An early influence was Tony Booth's writing on integration, including a short piece on integration in Italian schools. That made me think about cultural differences, and that made me interested in studying integration in different countries.

The central ideas in my book, on which my writings on disability have elaborated, are as follows. That policy is political, that politics shift, that ideas such as justice, democracy, or inclusion, guarantee nothing, that good intentions are not enough (Weber, Tomlinson applied to special education), that discourse is central to understanding and revealing people's assumptions and objectives, it is central to political life at all levels, and that people may have the same objectives but seek to achieve it using different terms (see the disagreement between the use of disabled in the British and Australian branches of the Disabled People's International).

Discourse is the analysis of language. 'Discourses deploy . . . various themes, styles of statements and . . . different objectives' (Fulcher, 1989, p. 4).Discourse is central to integration struggles. This is because ' Discourses articulate the world in certain ways: they "identify" problems, perspectives on those problems and thus "solutions" . . . [they] contain . . . a theory which informs practice, [which] means that we act on the basis of our ideas about how something works and what we want to achieve' (*ibid.,* p. 8). Discourse is tactic and theory. If we become too strident in emphasizing our discourse, however, we may not achieve our ends. Subtlety in practice, a sophistication about distancing ourselves from legislative and regulatory solutions – as I found in my literature research for the book, and in a later visit to Denmark – may serve us better. Moreover, discourse is a limited tool. Literature can sometimes serve us better. Peter Carey's novel, *The Unusual Life of Tristan Smith*, breaks most of the taboos about disability, and shows us life in its complexity. It is, I think, also a profound critique of the corporate world, the university and its sometimes well-intentioned agendas (Fulcher, 1998).

# Profile

## Bob Lingard

### *University of Queensland, Australia*

### Sample text

The Disadvantaged Schools Programme: caught between literacy and local management of schools (1998)

### Major influences

I come from a poor family. Both my mother and father left school early. They didn't have any secondary education. I'm the oldest of all the grandchildren. My brother, sister and I all went to this little primary school that my dad went to. We always did well and my parents used to say to the three of us that 'You are not going to be like us. You are all going to university'. My dad was a motor mechanic and I can't do anything practical because he wouldn't let me. He used to say, 'You're not going to lie on concrete floors under cars. You're going to wear white shirts and ties'. So it was all that respectable working-class and living through your kids – what Bennett and Cobb referred to as 'the hidden injuries of class'. We were born just after the Second World War and in Australia there was an education boom then and there were many more openings for males at that time. So the life I've had and the opportunities that I've had have come from a particular historical moment, as much as anything else. My son's life is totally different, a middle-class life with high expectations. When I went to university I was terrified; I was the first in my family to go and in the first instance I was alienated by the implicit cultural capital required in many of the subjects I took in my BA degree.

My parents were political to the extent that they were always on the side of the disadvantaged. That is deeply ingrained in me. I had teachers who sponsored and supported me through school and I'm basically where I am now both because of my parents and because of what those teachers did for me as a person. I feel enormously privileged.

I taught in schools for five or six years, in particular in a school with a high Aboriginal population in rural Australia. Some of the best kids I had in those classes were Aboriginal kids who are now in jail or don't have any jobs. Some of the non-Aboriginal kids who weren't so good academically are very successful. What I always tried to do when I was teaching was to say that, irrespective of where the kids were going to end up, they all had to be respected as human beings and they had to participate in society and have opinions and views.

## Quotations from sample texts

The Disadvantaged Schools Programme (DSP) is the longest-running Commonwealth equity programme in Australian schooling. It was established in 1974 by the Whitlam government as a cornerstone of the federal government's attempt to improve equality of educational opportunity for those students disadvantaged by socio-economic circumstances. While the programme had 'family resemblances' with equity programmes developed in other countries at about the same time, notably Headstart in the USA and the Education Priority Area programme in England, this was an idiosyncratically Australian programme. It differed from the former in its focus on whole-school change and reconstituted school and community relations and from the latter in its mediation by federalism in schooling.

(1998, p. 1)

At both federal and state levels of policy production, there has been a shift from an emphasis on increasing expenditure to a stress on improved outcomes at constant (or reducing) levels of funding. This emergent policy regime means that DSP schools have less capacity to utilize specific DSP funds for whole-school changes deemed necessary to improve educational outcomes for their students. The federal reconstitution of the DSP as a literacy programme for low socio-economic students, in effect, reduces the capacity for DSP schools and their communities to make judgements as to the best use of the funds at the school site. At the same time, with school-based management there is potentially less 'system support' – consultants, professional development, resource materials, research, and so on – for schools working with disadvantaged students.

To this point, the DSP has been the mainstay of equity programmes in Australian schooling. Much has been learnt in that time about the relationships between poverty and education. There is the potential in the new Commonwealth policy regime for those lessons to be totally forgotten and for the return of an individual deficit subject explanation of the poor performance of a disproportionate percentage of students from low socio-economic backgrounds. There is also the potential for narrowing the sort of schooling such students get access to. The market approach to schooling most likely will increase differentiation of provision within the government system and across the government/non-government divide. And all of this is occurring at the same time as an economy in transition results in greater social and economic inequalities and collapsed and reconstituted labour markets.

(1998, pp.11–12)

There is a continuing need for educational systems to target extra funds for schools with concentrations of low socio-economic students as part of their responsibility for the education of all students. This remains very important in the context of school-based management where schools are apparently only responsible for their students and in the context of a quasi-educational market where parents are only concerned with the schooling of their own children. However, there is a need to ensure that the targeting of funds in this way does not quarantine the issues from consideration across the system, creating tensions between inclusive practices at the school level and exclusionary practices at the system level. At the same time, there is a need to ensure teacher ownership and development of projects in disadvantaged schools aimed at whole-school change and more inclusive relationships with students and communities. Discretionary, yet targeted, funds for schools under a programme such as the DSP are important in that respect. While schools cannot compensate for society, they can make some difference.

(1998, p. 12)

## Reflections on inclusive education

I am really interested in the words 'inclusive education', to be honest, because in the Australian context inclusion came out of special education and was almost a synonym for 'mainstream'. That is, in Australia inclusion refers by and large to the 'mainstreaming' of 'special education' kids in ordinary schools. So it is interesting now that in Europe and the UK there is discussion about the words 'inclusion' and 'exclusion'. Those words are sort of coming into the policy lexicon in Australia but not in the same way.

I come out of an interest in kids from poor families and how schooling could be more inclusive there. I also come out of the gender question, both at a school level but much more at policy development. I've been interested in Australia in seeing how the word 'inclusion' can be seen in a broader, more encompassing way than simply a 'mainstreaming special education' definition. I've been involved in a research project which has got me interested in thinking about inclusion. This is a European Union one, EGSIE (Educational Governance and Social Inclusion and Exclusion). They allowed us to do an Australian comparative study. What I find interesting in these meetings is the huge range of meanings of 'inclusion' and 'exclusion'. In the Australian context, I thought the word 'inclusion' might be able to reconstitute social justice and equity agendas, and perhaps revitalize them. I am working on the new Equity Framework for the Queensland Department of Education. I was interested in trying to get inclusion on that agenda in its broadest sense: the special education aspect but also in relation to Aboriginal students, girls and working-class students. What we're trying to do is to get a charter where the State Department of Education will make statements of their commitment to special education kids, kids living in poverty, to indigenous kids, to recent migrant kids, and so on. They will set targets for their improved educational outcomes.

In some of the European definitions, there are some really narrow notions of 'inclusion' which equate it with 'employability'. I see it as being all-encompassing, linked to discrimination in relation to funding and allowing all people to be able to become fully active citizens. My head of department at the University of Queensland is in the State Department at the moment as Director General of Education for Queensland for six months. We've been trying to use 'social capital' notions there. I was taken aback recently when I was trying to develop this Equity Framework for the State Department. There were people who were Directors of Special Education in the State Department who became confused in the way we were using the language of 'inclusion' in relation to social justice. I see that as one of the strengths of Roger Slee's journal, the *International Journal of Inclusive Education*; that is, it attempts to use the concept in a broad fashion. There is a danger that if you push it out into multiculturalism, inclusion can also become an assimilation for uniformity rather than inclusion for diversity. So, there are questions about all that, 'Inclusion on whose terms?' and 'Who says you are to be included?' The Aboriginal people in Australia, for example, argue that they want more than tolerance and they want more than inclusion. They want both a recognition of difference and to be included. What I want to do is to hold to a broader definition which links across to the whole social justice, equity and citizenship issues. The concept of inclusion might also encourage an across-government approach to social and economic disadvantage.

## Links with different theoretical models

Sociology of education has always been my area. I was quite involved in Australia in the Disadvantaged Schools Programme, set up in the 1970s and which still exists today. It comes from the federal level and puts extra money in schools with a concentration of poor kids, basically.

Roger Slee and his attitude to inclusion has influenced me and also the inclusive curriculum of the Labor government policy in Queensland. An academic in Australia called Eva Cox – who did the equivalent of the UK 'Reith lectures', called the Boyer lectures in Australia – used the notion of 'social capital' to argue that policy and government had to be about the development of social capital. She was referring to the goals of education as being social as well as economic, as being about creating active citizens, social trust and creative conceptions of both community and nation.

# Profile

## *Peter Mittler*
### *Professor emeritus, University of Manchester, UK*

## Sample texts

Purposes and principles of assessment (1973)

Special needs education: an international perspective (1995)

Advocates and advocacy (1996)

## Major influences

I was working in the early 1960s in a hospital for autistic children and I wanted to explore the possibility of some of these children going to ordinary schools. It didn't strike me at the time as revolutionary. I was a clinical psychologist and the whole team, including social workers and nursing staff, wanted to try to include the children from the hospital in mainstream schools. I thought everyone was doing it. Then I realized it was extremely rare. So that was a major influence on the education side, which took me into ordinary schools. While I continued to work in the health service, there were several paediatricians who were major influences on my thinking. The academic, Jack Tizard, was a particular influence. He knew that change was possible. In the 1960s Manor Hospital in Epsom was a beacon of excellence where psychologists were using their skills and their knowledge of learning to help people with learning difficulties to learn. I saw that and it opened my eyes to what psychologists could actually do. I think that was what got me interested in clinical psychology. Mel Ainscow is a major influence on me now and I am very committed to his way of thinking. I was influenced by the American 'Headstart' research in the late 1960s. You have to set it in a historical context which was a personal one for me because the 'Headstart' work coincided with my arrival in Manchester to direct the Hester Adrian

102

Centre for research on children with learning difficulties and I went to America to look at research on 'mental retardation', as they called it there. What I learned about was early intervention and that severe poverty and disadvantage were not a barrier to parental participation. I remember being completely nonplussed by the fact that they were evaluating Headstart by the use of IQ tests, and IQ tests were still heavily used in England but they were already going out in America. The follow-ups show tremendous implications for policy because, although their IQs didn't change much, what did change was their social confidence and their self-esteem and they had a low conviction rate in the courts. I feel that there is still great pessimism about the ability of poorer people to become involved in their children's development.

## Quotations from sample texts

The revival of public, political and professional concern with the care and treatment of the mentally handicapped has led to a renewed insistence on adequate assessment, not only for its own sake, but as the basis of a programme of treatment in the broadest sense. Psychologists are not well prepared to meet this demand, partly because the mentally handicapped confront them with problems for which traditional assessment techniques seem inadequate if not actually irrelevant. Thus the incorporation into the educational system of some 35,000 severely handicapped children should act as a catalyst to a reconsideration of the psychologist's role, to a crystallisation of an already existing awareness of the limitations of traditional procedures, and to an increasing readiness to experiment with new methods.

(1973, p. 12)

Campaigns to include all disabled children in education are now an integral part of the comprehensive United Nations *Education for All* programmes. While this is ideologically and strategically advantageous, there is a real risk that disabled children in general and those with severe learning disabilities in particular will once again find themselves at the end of the line or even overlooked altogether.

We know from bitter experience that the needs of people with learning disabilities are usually the last to be included in a programme of educational reform and that there are still industrialised countries where they are excluded from any form of schooling and remain the responsibility of health or social welfare departments. Despite substantial progress in reaching and teaching such children, less that one per cent of those with significant learning disabilities attend any form of school in most developing countries (UNESCO, 1995). The rest remain at home, often leading lonely and isolated lives.

Advocates for people with learning disabilities need to take advantage of generic and comprehensive international initiatives such as *Education for All*, *Health for All* and the *International Year of the Family*. They should lobby hard both at the political and committee levels in the United Nations, and at their national governments, in order to ensure that the interests of the learning disabled are not overlooked and, in addition, that positive benefits result from such initiatives.

(1995, p. 105)

The most powerful and the most convincing advocates for change are people with learning disabilities themselves. Their advocacy can be expressed by creating an organization through movements like People First; alternatively or additionally, self-advocacy groups can be formed wherever groups of people are already meeting for other purposes, such as a day centre or residential centre or even a school or it can be developed by people coming together from different settings to form local groups. Self-advocacy can remain at the level of the individual making choices and decisions where real alternatives are seen to be available – and this process can begin and be encouraged in early childhood.

At the other end of the scale from grass-roots self-advocacy, there is a pressing need in all countries for appropriate legislation which ensures that the rights and needs of persons with learning disabilities are met and which actively counters discrimination. Very few countries have achieved this and the UK has a shameful record of its government's blocking at least 15 attempts to put such legislation on the statute book. This record is particularly disappointing since support for such legislation has come from the majority of parliamentarians and is also supported by the general public and all the relevant professional associations.

However, much of the force behind lobbies such as those wishing to pass anti-discrimination legislation has come from people with physical and sensory impairments. People with learning disabilities are now beginning to make common cause with people with other disabilities and are uniting in a single lobby. But there is still a long way to go before organizations and lobbies in this field include all people with disabilities and before those with learning disabilities demand and are given their rightful place in this movement.

(1996, pp. 13–14)

## Reflections on inclusive education

I find myself now to the left of the Green Paper, because I feel that they fudged the issue. I understand exactly why they fudged the issue. The Labour Party is much more committed to inclusive education than it was when in opposition. I worked with them then and I was in despair about the shilly-shallying. What they have written now in the Green Paper I agree with but I would like it to go further. My position on inclusive education now is that I am still not prepared to advocate the closure of special schools but I am nearer to it than I was. The position that I now take is that we have to start with the assumption of mainstream education for every child that is coming into the system. The LEA and educational psychologists have to assume that any child identified as having special educational needs will go to mainstream education. That has got to be the first assumption. Then the onus is on those doing the assessing, and that includes the parents of the child, to prove that this is not appropriate for the time being. This is not just because the child has Down syndrome or whatever but because the resources of the particular local school are inadequate. In the case of a child with physical impairments, you can actually spell out what is needed and I think that should really help.

One of the things which has changed my thinking on inclusion has been seeing young people with Down syndrome, whom I have known since they were babies, successfully make it through to secondary education, getting a handful of GCSEs. I know it is only a small number but each year the number increases. It is a sort of 'Road to Damascus' experience opening my local free newspaper and seeing a picture of a young person with Down syndrome who I knew when she was in our early intervention project who has now got six GCSEs. It shows what is now possible in inclusive education.

I used to be committed to the idea of each child having an individual integration plan (in addition to an individual education plan) so they could start off at special school but have planned periods in mainstream on a gradualist model. I now have less faith in the gradualist model. I was trained as a psychologist in gradualism, step-by-step rehabilitation of people out of long-stay hospitals into the community. Then I came across some research in America on supported employment, which made me realize that there were better models. This is called the 'Direct Placement Model' and it started with employment and can work towards education as well. On this model of rehabilitation, the question is 'Where do you want this person to finish?' You then place them there but provide high levels of support which can then be gradually withdrawn if the person can manage without it.

I still think the main barrier to inclusive education is attitude. If someone had said to me, when I was training as a clinical psychologist, the day will come before you retire when people with Down syndrome will get GCSEs, or the day will come when you will be invited by people with Down syndrome to their meeting which they will chair and run, I would have thought they were being 'unrealistic'. But in fact that is precisely what has happened. Let's get away from the word 'attitude'. The chief obstacle is underestimation. The biggest handicap that people with special needs have is our underestimation of their abilities.

## Links with different theoretical models

I don't actually think the deficit theory is wrong. You have to recognize that a lot of children have things wrong with them, very serious things. I don't go along with this complete dismissal of the deficit theory as necessarily bad. But, of course, it is completely inadequate as a theory to explain children's learning development. So in that sense the social model of disability needs to be addressed. We seem to have a lack of contact between theoretical work relating to children and theoretical work on adult disability.

My thinking has been enormously affected by the rights perspective. I have got that from disabled adults, not from working in special education. I think it is a human right for all children to be in regular schools.   But really that is not what is making the running. The running is being made by adult disabled people, not so far by people with learning disabilities but by people with physical and sensory impairments.

# Profile

## Brahm Norwich
### University of Exeter, UK

### Sample texts

*Reappraising Special Needs Education* (1990)

Has special educational needs outlived its usefulness? (1993a)

Ideological dilemmas in special needs education: practitioners'
views (1993b)

*Can Effective Schools be Inclusive Schools?* (Lunt and Norwich, 1999)

### Major influences

My father was a doctor and a surgeon and I come from a very medical
world, rather traditional. I graduated in the early 1970s and although I
was not particularly politically active I was very influenced by the student
movement, the whole questioning of values and lifestyle. I guess coming
from South Africa has been a big influence as well. I think, too, that my
visual problems had a big effect – I had serious eyesight difficulties from
about the age of ten, which led to two corneal grafts in my mid-twenties.

My initial and continuing interest has always been in psychologies that
had a strong applied element . . . I have been more interested in being a
practitioner than an academic. However, my interests were also in
philosophy and social and political matters. I had quite a lot of contacts
with clinical psychologists and I used to work in child guidance, but I was
always very interested in family therapy work and in community work,
and I was highly influenced by what people used to call 'community child
psychology'. It's the thought of getting out of the clinic and it was an
ambition to get into society to do home visits more, get into school more.

I think I was influenced when I started to work at the University of London Institute of Education by Klaus [Wedell]'s ideas. Klaus went from a sort of 'within-child' cognitive approach, to a sort of behaviour analytic framework, quite radical and very functional . . . I liked the functionalism of it . . . At the time [I was] very uneasy about psychometrics, and this provided an alternative. There is a side of me that is functional and practical, and there is a side of me which is more pensive; things are more ambiguous, open ended, exploratory.

The book that really changed my views I [first] read as an A-level student, *Sane Society* by Fromm, a Marxian psychoanalyst. Erich Fromm took an interdisciplinary view combining psychodynamic and social-economic conflict models. He did not deny the importance of the intrapsychic, or of character or personality or macro-social factors. I found these views insightful and expressing of a realistic humanity which appealed to me. So in a sense I thought 'I want to be like him . . .'; so my career choice to become a psychologist. I'd say George Kelly was also an influence, I was always interested in construct psychology. I liked Kelly, because of [his] theoretical pragmatism . . . and because he represents interactions between the different and opposing systems. I [also] read Freud and his ideas really attracted me . . . and I'm equally keen on Dewey, and Richard Rortie. [Philosophically] more recently I have been very impressed by Isaiah Berlin's conflict oriented liberalism.

## Quotations from sample texts

One way of summarising the main theme of this book is in terms of a commonly found style of dichotomous thinking in this field. I have tried to argue that thinking in terms of global oppositions and polarities between positions oversimplifies matters. This is not to imply that there are no answers to questions or working resolutions to basic dilemmas. It is rather to suggest that understanding derives from seeing connections and complementarity between positions, although there may be continuing tensions between them. This is most relevant to some of the social value positions taken in this and the wider educational field. This understanding can lead to an appreciation that dignity in learning for all does not depend only on equality, but can also arise from being treated as having autonomy and through some sense of belonging to a valued learning community.

(1990, p. 167)

The perspectives on special educational needs which I have discussed represent tension between two fundamental interpretations:
1. that special needs education is additional and different to ordinary provision
2. that ordinary provision is not accommodating to the diversity of individual needs.

Both interpretations capture significant aspects of what is involved in the field of providing for pupil diversity. But neither is sufficient without the other. This can be understood by considering the concept of SEN as a way of resolving conceptually the dilemma of identifying and providing for diversity. The tension arises from the existence of the negative social value placed in impairments and difficulties, on one hand, and the scarcity of provision and difficulties in managing provision, on the other. Stigma and devaluation can be avoided by including pupils into the mainstream, but that runs into scarcity and management limitations.

Of course, this is to put the tension in a stark and simple way, and there are in practice more and less effective ways of finding a balance. But my contention is that no final resolution to this dilemma is in view. This has, therefore, to be faced, digested and lived with. It means that a complex concept like SEN, despite its usefulness, is problematic. It also means that the interpretation of the concept as ordinary provision not accommodating individual needs is only part of the matter. This interpretation looks forward to special educational needs no longer existing at some future time, when full diversity can be accommodated. However, for as long as and to the extent that ordinary provision cannot accommodate, there will be the need for additional and different provision – there will be special educational needs in the other sense.

(1993a, p. 55)

If this study has highlighted the way in which decisions in this field involve ideological considerations and take on the form of resolving dilemmas, then there are certain implications. I suggest that it implies the value of accepting this fundamental feature, not resisting or denying it. However, there is no definitive statement of dilemmas in this field and the content of dilemmas would change over time. Nor is this stance one that leads to despair and a lack of direction. By accepting and living with the dilemmatic nature of decision making, we can adopt a more mature, committed and flexible approach to these very problems. We can also avoid practical solutions which are false resolutions because they fail to consider the possible positive and negative consequences of certain ways forward. Of course, we cannot make progress, merely by thinking in different ways. For that, we need the resources of commitment and endurance, which in practice means more finance.

(1993b, p. 545)

We have come to the conclusion that with the current dominant conception of effectiveness, we cannot say, yes, effective schools are inclusive ones. We have shown that this is partly to do with contemporary definitions of effectiveness as non-inclusive of the full diversity. We have also illustrated in the analysis of 1998 GCSE results that the schools achieving the highest GCSE results were not those where we found the higher concentrations of pupils with more and less severe SEN. One could even ask whether schools which focus so strongly on maximising 5 A–C GCSEs in the current competitive climate are likely to be welcoming and conducive places for children with difficulties in learning? But, should not our concept of the most 'effective' or 'best' schools be broad enough for it to incorporate inclusiveness? Is inclusion not the heart of 'good' or 'effective' education? Not so, was our conclusion. Inclusion is a very important value in education, but not the only value in education. Just as important is quality teaching that addresses individual needs. In accepting that there are multiple and contrary values in education, we need to resolve dilemmas by finding optimal balances and trade-offs. We have also argued that it is too easy to slip into talking about effective and inclusive schools as if these are straight-forward and identifiable characteristics of schools. Our conclusion is that it is more valid to talk about schools that are effective in relation to specific criteria, for specific groups of pupils and at a particular period of time. Similarly, schools might be inclusive in some respects and not others. Both effectiveness and inclusiveness are heavily value-laden concepts. They bring us back to basic questions about aims and values in education. We need to constantly remember this and continue to be alert to attempts to reduce questions of education and schooling merely to technical and empirical questions.

(1999, p. 84)

## Reflections on inclusive education

Special needs is an important concept with various elements – individuality, additionality and difference. In the end it's a legislative term, of course, about resources . . . but a very important concept in trying to work out some very hard decisions about what's most appropriate for individuals and their individuality. My ideas on special needs have changed, they've loosened up but I still have some deep uncertainties about models. I've spent quite a bit of time trying to counter what I see as over-simple theories, and particularly views that are too singular and blinkered. I think that radical inclusion is not as simple as it is made out to be; I think it smacks of a kind of hidden authoritarianism, in the way in which concealed interests take up supposedly very humane ideas.

For me there is a fundamental issue here about the nature of education – how much of it is for social purposes and how much for individual purposes, and the tensions between them. My reservations about inclusion are about those people who see education too much in the social and deny the individual . . . I guess that's what my views are about – ideological dilemmas! . . . and I don't go for the so-called 'third way' because that is a sort of trivialization of a deep tension that people actually need to experience, feel uncomfortable with and play out. The dominant political discourse of New Labour imports terms that put people's minds to sleep. Giddens (1997) reduces equality into the terms of inclusion, and I think that is a very risky move, because it suppresses the tensions. It fails to recognize different kinds of resolutions and that in the end no one value will predominate.

My current view on inclusion is that it is not useful to talk about education and put 'inclusion' in front of it, because that almost prejudges what education is about. When we talk about 'special educational needs', the whole of education is not referenced. A good education will address issues of inclusion and equality and participation, but there is a tension between education from the point of view of society, and education from the point of view of the individual; so I tend to argue that there are limits to inclusion that are not just practical but that there are ethical limits, which come about through the learner's expressing a choice, or parents expressing a preference, or communities expressing a preference which might not go along with what a larger group might think is in the interests of those people. Autonomy, individuality and preference (if not choice) are linked and crucial social values with relevance to education including the education of students with disabilities and difficulties.

## Links with different theoretical models

A part of the problem with psychology has been that some strands have denied the social and ethical debates; denying the moral and social order. [On the other hand] I think the sort of mantras of 'celebrating diversity' are too simple. I don't think that that phrase captures all of what disability is about; there is a lot of pain and suffering in disability; disability is a much more complex issue than recent social models [can allow for].

[Anyway] all psychologists believe in a kind of social model; if you're a behaviourist you believe in the micro-social rather than a macro-social model; if you're a classical Freudian you'd probably agree with the social model of experience, so the notion of what is social seems to me to be very undertheorized. 'Who doesn't believe in the social model?', is what I would say, and the dichotomizing between medical and social models is nonsense; medical models are medical models, and anyone who knows anything about medicine will know that there are the hard-line biomedical models, but then you get the more socio-medical models.

Individuality is so important; the risk in a bureaucracy is that you treat everyone uniformly and their individuality is overlooked and that's the worst risk in the poorly theorized social models, a form of authoritarianism.

# Profile

## *Mike Oliver*
### *University of Greenwich, UK*

### Sample texts

*The Politics of Disablement* (1990)

Changing the social relations of research production? (1992)

### Major influences

I didn't go through a special school, so I have no experience of special schools at first hand. Obviously, as a lecturer in special education I spent quite a lot of time visiting students in special schools. I also know a lot of people who did spend all their formative years in special schools. I know of the pain and damage that was done and the consequences for many people now in their fifties and sixties who are still living with the inheritance of that. So my conviction is that there is no place for special education in the world in the twenty-first century. It is reinforced, not on the basis of me having bad experiences personally in special schools, but in terms of what I have seen and what I know. I think the whole issue about my own experiences as a disabled person in terms of how that has influenced my thinking as a sociological theorist and a political activist may be one of the reasons I am interested in male country and western singers. They always sing about the road and the train. They are always on a journey to somewhere. I think I've been on a journey as well, in which my own understanding of myself has changed. You know, I started out 25 years ago as a typical academic, saying 'Let's be objective. Let's study the world'. I was advised not to get into disability because it was too personal. Then I moved into recognizing that personal experience gives you an added dimension to use to authenticate the work. Then I moved on to feeling that it is not an adequate model in itself either, because you are what you are. You've got to embrace rather than merely use what you are. So it is a journey from being objective and exclusionary to authenticity, then through to embracing with pride, that I have been on.

My previous background had been in sociology and social work at the University of Kent, where I had done my undergraduate degree, my PhD and then later worked as a lecturer. I was on a three-year contract and when it came to an end I had no choice other than to apply elsewhere and I got this job as a lecturer in special education, and so came into it that way: not quite through the back door but through the side door as a sociologist.

My invention and development of the social model of disability was not something that I thought up out of my own head. It was really a response to a need to teach 'the fundamental principles of disability' (UPIAS, 1976) to trainee social workers in a way they would understand. So that was a massive influence. I think on top of that Finkelstein's (1980) book *Attitudes and Disabled People* and particularly the kind of materialistic, historical slant that he put on the whole issue of disability: a lot of my work subsequently has been an attempt to build on and define that. Something more specifically in special education was Sally Tomlinson's (1982) book *A Sociology of Special Education* which had an impact on what I did. Prior to that, there was no sociology in special needs, there was no kind of discussion that went beyond medicine, psychology and education. By the time I moved into special education, there was this whole kind of aura about Sally's book which almost said it should be burned. Sally herself was kind of demonized by some teachers. I was just frankly amazed and staggered at the anger that this book had raised in special education. It wasn't saying anything that we didn't already know. It was just basically saying that special education is shaped by a variety of interests and, as a consequence of that, it doesn't always end up benefiting those it claims to benefit. I never cease to be surprised in many ways at the arrogance of the teaching profession, which is only matched by the arrogance of the medical profession, and I think it is very different from some other professions like social work, occupational therapy and physiotherapy.

## Quotations from sample texts

In attempting to develop a social theory of disability within a sociological framework, it is necessary to stress what is and what is not being attempted. It is not the intention to use the category 'disability' to resolve disputes within sociology itself, whether they be about economic determinism, relative autonomy, ideology or whatever else. Rather the intention is more limited; to show that disability as a category can only be understood within a framework, which suggests that it is culturally produced and socially structured.

(1990, p. 22)

Disability cannot be abstracted from the social world which produces it; it does not exist outside the social structures in which it is located and independent of the meanings given to it. In other words, disability is socially produced. In the past 100 years or so, industrial societies have produced disability first as a medical problem requiring medical intervention and second as a social problem requiring social provision. Research, on the whole, has operated within these frameworks and sought to classify, clarify, map and measure their dimensions.

The late twentieth century has seen a crisis develop in these productions of disability because disabled people have recognised the medical and individual ideologies underpinning them. What is more, having done so, they are now engaged in a struggle to produce disability as social oppression. As this struggle continues and disabled people grow in strength, the crisis in disability production will deepen and researchers will be forced to answer the question Howard Becker posed 30 years ago: whose side are you on? Such are the fundamentals with which we are now dealing.

(1992, p. 101)

## Reflections on inclusive education

When I went on to the Fish Committee as part of the team  reviewing provision to meet special educational needs in Inner London (Fish, 1985a), it was a compromise between all of us who sacrificed our principles to come out  with a consensus where we all tried to make sure it said the things we wanted it to say but none of us wanted to upset the people that we had grown fond of and had worked with in the previous 12 months. I think we all have that kind of struggle. As Linden Johnson said, 'Do you want to be inside the tent pissing out or outside the tent pissing in?' When I went on to the Fish Committee I decided for a while I'd be inside the tent pissing out. When I became a non-executive director of a health trust, I spent another period of my life inside the tent pissing out. But I suppose I feel more comfortable outside the tent pissing in.  But equally, it involves some kind of struggle. For example, I give the introductory lecture to visiting Dutch students and I am conscious that I want the lecture to say that special education is bad and therefore all of you are oppressors and there is a sense in which I actually believe that. That is not a very helpful thing to tell students on their first day on a course. One has to say things which do justice to the complexities and which don't denigrate the very real commitments which lots of people put into their professional practice, not simply to build careers and pay their mortgages but because they are genuinely committed to working for the children in their schools. I think inevitably all we can do is live with those contradictions.

Professionally, it is not recognized or acknowledged that disabled people have any voice, even where it is recognized they have a view. It is always denigrated by the argument that 'Well, that might have been how it was when you went to special schools, but it has changed now and we are not really taking about the same thing'. I think there is an enormous wealth of experience and pain out there which special education has not yet acknowledged. Getting into and opening up some of that is one of the priorities in terms of beginning to move special education away from the way it is going at the moment.

Current discourses around integration or inclusion are still professionally led. While the words have changed, the reality hasn't. Integration is still a lot of professionals, with power, talking about the issue of special educational needs, as if there are no other important stakeholders who are involved. Everyone is an integrationist now. It is just that we're not all using the word in the same way.

I really don't mind if someone in the pub on a Saturday night uses the word 'handicapped'. I might mind if someone uses that word in an academic paper but I really don't care on a Saturday night. I don't see it as my job to police that kind of thing. People use the vocabularies that are available to them which are not intended to be hurtful or harmful. The struggle for language should continue but we should be selective about the sites and battlegrounds where we fight over language. I think when we do we should do it with humour and good sense and we should avoid some of the extremes of PC (political correctness) which are often not about activists engaged in struggles. They are often about counter-activists seeking to rubbish legitimate struggles, so we need to recognize that element as well.

## Links with different theoretical models

A visiting lecturer in disability studies from New Zealand said to me: 'If Karl Marx was the founding father of sociology, then Mike Oliver is the founding father of disability studies.' I think in many ways I have been lucky in that I was able to build on the bedrock of the fundamental principles from Vic Finkelstein's work and to take them further when nobody else was doing it. There are difficulties with the second generation of disability theorists as they now come up. What do you do, in psychoanalytical terms, in order to progress? Do you have to kill your father first? I think there is some stuff going on where disability theory can forget that, for the vast majority of disabled people throughout the world, life is pretty awful. First and foremost disability theory ought to be about people having control over their own bodies before we get on to concerns about the way in which media images represent disabled people. If we are not careful, in 10 or 15 years time this thing called 'disability studies' will be an elite group of disabled people talking among themselves about how they are represented in culture, while the rest of disabled people continue to die or to empty their bowels at other people's request rather than when they are ready to do it themselves.

I think I have a particular place in bringing disability into sociological theory. I have made policy-makers aware that disabled people themselves have a lot to contribute to the policy-making process. My work has made a contribution to professionals to think about what they are doing and maybe, in some cases, to begin to develop different ways of doing things. The aspect of my work which I am most proud of is my contribution to the collective rather than the individual empowerment of disabled people. I have laid a basis for the disability movement to collectively organize in the struggle against oppression.

The two things that are most important to me are that I am a sociologist and a political activist and the book published in 1990, *The Politics of Disablement* is the one that most adequately straddles both of these areas. It is the one that still sells more copies than my other books.

# Profile

## *Patricia Potts*
### *Canterbury Christchurch University College, UK*

### Sample texts

Did they all get into the ark? (1987)

Gender and membership of the mainstream (1997)

Human rights and inclusive education in China: a western
  perspective (1999)

### Major influences

I went to a school where everybody had passed the 11-plus but in which
most people felt inadequate, so selection was a huge and daily issue. When
the school had its centenary, the local newspaper had a photograph of a
group of students from a past generation and the article was headed 'The
could-do-better girls'. So, there are links obviously between my education
as a school student and my subsequent interest in the uses and abuses,
successes and failures of educational attainment levels.

Had my teacher training been more imaginative or more politically
explicit in its organization, I think I might still be a history teacher in a
mixed ability school. My disappointment with that training was one of the
reasons why I went to work in a junior training centre. There were lots of
ways in which it represented progress for the students in the school and
lots of ways in which it didn't. The experience of being in this lovely school
which was two honeycombs built around a hall and a swimming pool full
of light was a lot better than the hospital school that most of the children
had been bussed out to before the 1971 Education Act.

I grew up with a disabled father. This is a major dimension to my
upbringing but would never have been consciously in my mind as
meaning that I was interested in disability issues. It is not something that

I would have discussed at home. I remember one of my earliest memories is thinking that it is fairly peculiar for grown-up men to be able to walk, because my father could not walk. So you know it is there but it is not there, and I will never know how it affected my decision to not become a history teacher.

## Quotations from sample texts

The sorts of difficulties faced by some of Blackshaw's children include speech and language problems, behavioural and emotional problems and mild hearing-losses. Most ordinary pre-school groups include children who experience such problems, though not, usually, where they have been severe enough to be identified formally. Health-service personnel do not see the nursery as the right place for children who have already been given a 'handicap' label and tend to use a multi-professional diagnostic unit for children about whom there are serious worries. Identification can therefore be a ticket to special resources, but it also restricts a child's choice of pre-school group. Professionals are aware, however, of the consequences of segregated placements and are keen to support children in the ordinary nursery if their difficulties are seen as temporary, not 'constitutional'.

For children with marked physical or mental impairments they express a protective attitude, arguing that a special unit helps families to come to terms with this situation and meet up with others whose experiences are similar, while at the same time providing a more appropriate social life for their children. Whether or not this division of services for children reflects a 'natural' state of affairs or not could be debated, of course, for the planning that results in different kinds of provision reveals the attitudes and priorities of the planners rather than different kinds of humanity among children. Many professionals believe that specialized training and the concentration of resources immediately to hand are essential and justify the segregation of their consumers.

(1987, pp. 362–3)

The interrelationships between gender, disability, attainment and social role are complex. Consequently, the implications for the reduction of inequalities do not point to a single direction of change. Guaranteeing equality of access to and participation in mainstream educational communities for all female students and professional workers requires a transformation of the system. However, changes which threaten the space, culture, identity and survival of those with established or effective power are bound to be resisted. It seems to me therefore that positive discrimination is a necessary, non-violent strategy for modelling and implementing change.

For example, relevant systems of monitoring and support for both students and staff could be strengthened. These would include self-advocacy, self-assessment and more single-sex optional groupings within comprehensive educational settings. They would also include measures to provide managerial experience for disabled people, women and members of ethnic minorities. Accountability in appointments and promotions procedures would be a priority. Access to short-lists and the sharing of subsequent jobs would also increase the diversity of role models for the community as a whole.

We have seen that disruptive boys receive a disproportionate amount of resources. We have also seen that men are awarded a disproportionate number of promoted positions, even in educational settings where the majority of experienced workers are women. Neutralizing these aggressive behaviours would involve making more room for girls and women, literally as well as politically. A different approach to the use of space and time would transform the educational mainstream.

(1997, p. 184)

China and the West are officially committed to the view that access to education is a right. However, dominant ideologies in both China and the West support the development of specialized provision alongside the educational mainstream. Inclusive education is not seen as the right of all students, even where it is increasingly perceived as a positive goal for some groups.

In the West, rights can be seen as a record of past conflicts, charting the reduction of absolute, unelected power. In China, rights are non-negotiable. Conflicts of interest between groups of people are denied: the 'people' are indivisible. Power struggles cannot be publically acknowledged or resolved. The possibility of the abuse of power cannot be raised, except by those at the top. The position of both China and the West, however, is informed by an understanding that the assertion of civil rights is associated with bourgeois revolutions. In Britain this makes the middle classes the particular friends of the government; in China they are the particular enemies.

Neither Western nor Chinese values guarantee a democratic education system based on the values of social inclusion. If the obstacles seem to be greater in China because of the absence of political freedom and the rule of law, then the efforts of some educators to introduce the values of social justice into their schools must be seen as significant. In Western countries where there is official support for inclusion and freedom of choice, there is less excuse for educators to perpetuate educational inequalities.

(1999, p. 65)

## Reflections on inclusive education

Since the implementation of the 1981 Act I have done quite a lot of advocacy work with families. I have been to a number of appeals. I think working as a professional person with families, in their struggle to get what they want for their children, has been the most amazing source of understanding and experience for me. They think that when you work with them you are going to help them to raise their status sufficiently that they are going to have leverage. Of course, what you realize is that, in joining families, you give up some of your power. You reduce your power to work with them.

I had both my daughters while I was working at the Open University and that was one of the reasons I got involved in under-5s activities and community projects. Not only did I not want to write about inclusive education from an elitist university, I didn't want to write about inclusive education and encourage my children to go to exclusive schools. It is to do with the integration of my personal and professional life. I think my daughters understand that their education is a political one and that this has significantly shaped their experience.

Some of the practitioners that I talk to, working in major cities, feel optimistic about moving towards a more inclusive system. However, I see many barriers. I think that competition and selection have been shored up. I see that democracy is not seen as important or relevant to education. Somehow, things that we want in the rest of life are not acceptable to address in the context of school.

## Links with different theoretical models

I see that positivist models still dominate in educational research which I think is completely irrelevant. I see official language and terminology as unclear, perpetuating negative categorical thinking and reflecting a lack of commitment. It also reflects what I see as a contradictory orthodoxy, which is that inclusion and exclusion are both good for different sorts of students at different sorts of times. I think the language of inclusion has been hijacked by the government. I think there is progress towards a rights-based society in this country but there are huge barriers in education.

I feel I have worked to make links between inequalities of gender, race and class and inequalities in responding to difficulty in learning. They are to be brought together in the notion of participatory or inclusive education. I pursue a commitment to a social understanding of barriers to learning and how they might be overcome. I try to maintain a consistency between the content of my work, research methodology, professional setting and how this all relates to the rest of my life.

# Reflection

## Sheila Riddell
### *University of Glasgow, UK*

### Sample texts

Parents, professionals and social welfare models: the implementation of the Education (Scotland) Act 1981 (Riddell, Dyer and Thompson, 1990)

Parental power and special educational needs: the case of specific learning difficulties (Riddell, Brown and Duffield, 1994)

*Special Educational Needs Policy in the 1990s: Warnock in the Market Place* (Riddell and Brown, 1996)

The concept of the learning society for adults with learning difficulties: human and social capital perspectives (Riddell *et al.*, 1997)

Social capital and people with learning difficulties (Riddell, Baron and Wilson, 1999)

Captured customers: people with learning difficulties in the social market (Riddell, Wilson and Baron, 1999)

The meaning of the learning society for women and men with learning difficulties (Riddell, Baron and Wilson, forthcoming)

Special educational needs and competing policy frameworks in England and Scotland (Riddell *et al.*, forthcoming)

I started my working life as an English teacher in a comprehensive school in the south-west of England. Although hardly a hotbed of radical activity, the English department in which I worked was unusually progressive, teaching mixed ability classes throughout the school, and, at the same time, obtaining better examination results than any other department. For a novice teacher, fresh from a PGCE year at Sussex University, teaching groups of 14-year-olds studying science fiction, the genre of the Western and King Lear in the same classroom was surely demanding. However, what I learnt in the classroom had a profound and lasting influence on my later academic work. First, I learnt about the importance of clear communication in the written and spoken word. I have always tried to make my work accessible, believing that complex ideas can and should be communicated in as simple a manner as is possible to convey their meaning. Secondly, I felt that research should be connected with the world of policy and practice; it was important for researchers to think about the practical implications of their ideas and resist the temptation to be drawn into endless rounds of critical speculation with no touchstone in reality. In terms of substantive interests, two major concerns arose as a result of my classroom experience which weave in and out of my academic work. I encountered feminist ideas shortly after I started teaching and became very aware of the way in which the micro-politics of gender informed relationships in the classroom and staffroom. In the late 1970s, women teachers, influenced by the women's movement, were challenging overt and covert discrimination. Regarded within the school and by the LEA as somewhat deranged, there was none the less a wonderful sense of empowerment in pushing at apparently immovable structures and watching them shift.

For me, gender politics were never stand-alone but were always linked with those of class and 'ability'. Teaching completely mixed ability groups, it was none the less apparent that selection processes were still at work. We were able to avoid the damaging labelling of students in the early years, but by the time external examinations loomed, we were forced to decide which students were going to be entered for CSE and which for O-level. (In Scotland now the decision would be which level of Standard grade they would take). While, at one level, the sifting process was entirely meritocratic, I was very conscious of the permeating social class issues linked with constructions of (natural?) ability. Students from socially disadvantaged backgrounds were much less likely to be entered for O-level, and children with learning difficulties and behavioural difficulties were rarely from socially advantaged families. For many children with special educational needs, the experience of schooling was often isolating and lonely. Although we were attempting to include all children within a mixed ability classroom, and our teaching materials were differentiated to 'meet the needs of the individual child', none-the-less I had an uncomfortable feeling that external assessment was driving our teaching. Despite our best efforts to include them, those who were struggling with basic literacy and numeracy skills, particularly if quiet and undemanding, often remained untutored somewhere in the class with most educational experiences simply passing them by. Their major goal was to avoid teacher attention and hard pressed teachers concentrated their energies on those students who demanded their attention for behavioural or academic reasons.

After seven years at the school, I felt in need of a change of direction and enrolled for a PhD, in the School of Education at the University of Bristol on gender and option choice. The study included a particular group of pupils with special needs, taught separately in a remedial class, for whom little curricular choice existed due to the restricted curriculum they followed. My PhD was awarded in 1988, the same year as the Education Reform Act was enshrined in statute, removing some of the choices available to pupils which had been the focus of my PhD and instead establishing the parental choice as the central mechanism driving the introduction of the market into education.

In 1988, I moved to Scotland and worked for a year with Professor George Thomson at Edinburgh University on a study of the implementation of the post-Warnock legislation in Scotland. There were both positive and negative features of joining a three-year project for its last year, when both of the previous researchers had left. A large pile of unanalysed data had to be tackled and I had a steep learning curve both in terms of understanding the Scottish system and the expanding field of special educational needs. On the positive side, however, I found that not only was this area fascinating in its own right, but also offered the opportunity to explore competing social welfare models, as the dominant model of professional control was challenged by the growth of consumerism (Riddell, Dyer and Thomson, 1990). Competition between these two discourses, played out throughout the 1990s in England and Scotland, has been a recurring theme within my work and has been explored in relation to policy and practice for children with specific learning difficulties (Riddell, Brown and Duffield, 1994) and the management of assessment and recording (Riddell *et al.*, forthcoming). The seven years I spent working in the Department of Education at the University of Stirling gave me the opportunity to interact with teachers of learning support and special school teachers, who shared with me their first hand experiences of the impact of educational reform on special educational needs. Some of these experiences are reflected in a book I edited with Sally Brown (Riddell and Brown, 1996), which attempted an overview of the impact of marketization and managerialism in special needs education in England and Scotland.

I am currently working in the Strathclyde Centre for Disability Research at the University of Glasgow, located within a Department of Social Policy and Social Work and my research now focuses on the aspects of the restructuring of welfare in relation to disabled people. While much of this work deals with education, I also work in the areas of training, employment and their links with health and quality of life. With Stephen

Baron and Alastair Wilson, I have just completed a study in the ESRC Learning Society programme entitled 'The Meaning of the Learning Society for Adults with Learning Difficulties' (Riddell, Baron and Wilson, forthcoming). This research combined documentary analysis and an interview survey of lifelong learning provision for disabled people in Scotland with detailed ethnographic case studies, the latter providing insight into the ways in which service users experience the complex web of service provision delivered by a bewildering array of agencies. Perhaps our most striking finding is that, while all service providers talk about their commitment to normal life principles and the provision of mainstream opportunities, the reality is that most services continue to channel people with learning difficulties into 'special' tracks which segregate rather than include and empower care managers rather more than service users (Riddell, Baron and Wilson, 1999). We have explored the way in which human and social capital versions of a learning society are played out in the experiences of people with learning difficulties, the dominant human capital model meaning that investment in people tends to be commensurate with their perceived ability to contribute added value to the economy. While lifelong learning within a knowledge society is seen as the means of both economic and social regeneration, many socially marginalized groups may be further excluded by the expectation that each individual bears responsibility for maintaining their own employability (Riddell *et al.*, 1997; Riddell, Wilson and Baron, 1999). This study has also allowed us to explore sociological themes of negotiated risk and the construction of identity. Whereas postmodern writers like Ulrich Beck tend to emphasize the ability of the individual to engage in 'reflexive self-constitution', negotiating their identity and life-course with significant others, our work highlights the powerful influence of social class and gender as well as that of the master category of learning difficulties. This ascribed social status tends to negate other social advantages and may be used to justify the denial of basic political and human rights (Riddell, Baron and Wilson, forthcoming).

Over the next few years, I hope to continue exploring social policy themes in the areas of education, training and employment, questioning in particular the implications of New Labour's commitment to a particular form of public accountability informed by target-setting and audit. This will involve further thought about the ways in which research interacts both with the policy-making agenda but also, and more importantly, with the concerns of disabled people.

# Reflection

## Roger Slee
### University of Western Australia

### Sample texts

*Is There a Desk with my Name on It? The Politics of Integration* (1993)

Special education and human rights in Australia: how do we know about disablement and what does it mean for educators? (1999)

The challenge in trying to account for our intellectual development is to extract events, experiences, people and literature that stand as formative landmarks, and disregard the minutiae of that which we dismiss as the daily grind. However, on reflection the minutiae is the mortar that sets the formative bricks of a life. How do you start if not to describe the cultural lessons of life from family, from school, from the communities you move in and through. How do we come to know what we do? What tools are we given to interpret the world and imagine it otherwise?

Now that sounds grand, for the task I have been given is to think about how I came to position myself as an advocate for inclusive education, and to trace that in my writing. Serendipity figures large, but that reduces a life. Elsewhere, I have written about shame-full early encounters with disablement and the contribution of those experiences to a widely shared *common sense*.

> My own biography produces shameful memories. I recollect the way that my friends and I would break into a run as we passed Mullaratarong (many of the special centres were given Aboriginal names, but not I think as a sign of solidarity). It was necessary to run in order to avoid ending up like the kids inside. The mythology, an epistemic etching, exerted such power over us. Parents disabused us of the fear of contagion and adjusted our attitudes to an

125

attitude of pity. Thinking back it now occurs to me that I never saw any of the kids inside their purpose-built high fences. The point was, we didn't need to, we had knowledge about them revolving around loose conceptions of illness, deformity and above all else *abnormality*.

(Slee, 1999, pp. 123–4)

Rather than rehearse these early formations I propose to briefly think about some disruptive events and people, those that unsettled and suggested a not-so-common sense. Most of us, as Shapiro (1994) remarks just don't get it, we don't understand disabled people. This is hardly astonishing as our lessons are always at a distance. Such is the organization of our world that encounters with disabled people are few, incidental or accidental. After leaving school I used to go to a nursing home with my friend, now my partner, to visit some people who she had met in the spinal injuries ward at the Princess Alexandra hospital while her brother was there following a football injury. As conversation replaced my own ineptitude I had a sense that the world wasn't really as I knew it. There are depths to this story which continue. I will not plumb them here. Suffice to say these encounters created an opening, a crack for new intelligence.

Doing my Graduate Diploma of Education (PGCE) I was asked to teach about handicap (a rarely contested word at the time) in social studies. My supervisor told me to talk to Pam, another teacher at the school whose husband was reading for a PhD in sociology with a focus on disability. Pam arranged for me to meet her husband Ric. Ric used a wheelchair and led me through a very different set of theoretical precepts. He spoke of C. Wright Mills to distinguish between social issues and personal troubles, and distinguished between disability, impairment and handicap. I taught the unit, became a teacher and packed away Ric's notes.

Years later I was transferred to an inner urban high school in Melbourne which had been a selective high school and recognized as an elite school, the private school for state school kids. Kids there did rowing and the school had a large music department. It provided a narrow opening into the middle classes for some kids. I was promoted through the school. This effectively meant that I got an office where other teachers could send 'bad' kids for me to *discipline*. The same kids came each day from the same classes. I came to think that schools weren't meant for these kids. While I think I was correct in so much as these schools were designed to eject most kids as early as possible, I had forgotten about Ric and C. Wright Mills. My mission, and mission it was, was to fix these defective kids so we could get them back into what I never openly interrogated as dysfunctional institutions. The idea, and we didn't trouble ourselves to read the British report, *Behaviour Units* (HMI, 1978), to learn of their misgivings about their attempt at this project, was to teach the kids what they needed to know to survive in the classroom, to build their self-esteem and repertoire of coping strategies and then integrate them back into schools. For my theoretical sins I allowed myself to be transferred to a behaviour unit where I worked assiduously at kid-saving.

At the unit we spent a great deal of time in the company of psychologists, special education teachers, social workers and a range of other experts. They had a much better vocabulary than me. They really knew the problems of these kids, their diagnostic tools and charts gave them a professional authority that outstripped the hunch-ridden classroom teacher. I needed a graduate diploma of special education, I needed to know the defects of the kids. Until I could spell and pronounce aeteology, I was not really helping my *emotionally disturbed clients*.

The coincidence of a number of factors while working at the behaviour unit directed me towards a reading of inclusion that was counter to the prevailing view. First, the good fortune to be a student of Bob Semmens. Second, a growing frustration that our students never got to the successful re-entry into their old schools bit of the equation, coupled with a corresponding sense that as more units opened we were the *de facto* sector for the kids schools didn't want. Third, the publication of *Integration in Victorian Education* (Education Department of Victoria, 1984), a document that paradoxically proposed that all kids have a right to a place in their neighbourhood school.

A criminologist, Bob Semmens reminded me of the earlier lessons from C. Wright Mills and laid open in front of me the pages of work by Ken Polk, Art Pearl and Tony Knight to think differently about student discipline. He also suggested that I read *A Sociology of Special Education* (Tomlinson, 1982) and *Special Education: Policy, Practices and Social Issues* (Barton and Tomlinson, 1981). This literature led in two directions: a new sociology of education, and to the work of Mike Oliver, and in turn a whole chorus of disabled researchers' voices. From this point I decided that it was more important to be able to understand, pronounce and spell epistemology and I forgot about the diagnostic track.

The work at the unit was presenting me with deep ideological tensions. More of the kids referred to the unit came with a greater range of labels for us to sort and shelve. Yes the kids were difficult, disruptive, phobic about school, defective in academic skills; but what did this mean? I believed the immediate turn to them for individual pathological explanations let us off the hook. Why not explore the deep pathology of schooling?

The publication of the so-called Integration Report declared a conviction to increasing the participation of kids in regular schools as a right for all. Ironically, I worked at an educational terminus and with my colleagues attempted a slight of logic: 'Since they are not included at their regular school, let's pull them out, fix them up so that they can be included.' You can only say this so many times before you feel the crowd's eyes piercing your new 'emperorial' (regal) robes.

Shortly afterwards, in a new job. I realized that I was involved in a long struggle of cultural politics. I edited *Is There a Desk with my Name on It?* (Slee, 1993) following a conversation with one of my graduate students. She felt extreme comfort from the discussion of disability politics and education initiated for us by John Lewis, a critical educational historian. 'I recognised my daughter's teachers in that lot in there (her classmates who were also teachers)', she said. She then went on to tell me a tragic episode from her own biography concerning her daughter who had been 'integrated' into her local rural school. The child was encouraged by the teacher to rehearse in the school concert and was even told to make a costume for the performance. The parents, having spoken of nothing else with their daughter at meal times for weeks, sat in the auditorium as the lights dimmed and the costumed kids danced onto the stage. One child was not present. Distraught, the parents went backstage at the end of the evening to investigate. The teacher had kept the child backstage because she worried that the child would feel conspicuous as the only child with Down syndrome on the stage.

There is not much to say after that. My work since that time has essentially been dedicated to understanding how people come to think like that, why such thinking is sustained at professional and popular levels and how we can change it. My writing and research is about the link between the formation of knowledge and social exclusion. As Ann Oakley (2000, p. 8) puts it: 'Everybody thinks they know certain things, but debating what knowledge is and how to reach it has traditionally lain in the domain of experts.' Our struggle is to change the power relations of knowledge-authority, to consider whose voices carry weight and who never gets heard. As Ellen Brantlinger (1997) puts it, we are engaged in a task of 'speaking back to power'. Inclusive education rejects normalization, it is vehemently anti-assimilationist. This is cultural politics where disability is one aspect of a general discussion of the politics of identity and difference. I'm sermonizing. Did I mention being forced into the Sunday school classroom when other kids were allowed to play all weekend?

# Profile

## *Sally Tomlinson*
*University of Oxford, UK*

## Sample texts

*Special Education: Policy, Practices and Social Issues* (Barton and Tomlinson, 1981)

*A Sociology of Special Education* (1982)

Exclusion: the middle classes and the common good (1999)

## Major influences

From a sociological perspective, I was left of centre, a neo-Marxist and neo-Weberian. The sociology of education, throughout the 1950s, 1960s and 1970s, was demonstrating the perpetuation of inequalities throughout the education system. I was influenced by people like Steven Rose at the Open University, who was among the first to look at the pernicious influence of fixed notions of IQ. I go along, curiously enough, with Edward Boyle who was Conservative minister in 1960–62. He had this idea that you created intelligence and I think this is what we do. Many children don't have the opportunity for intelligence to be created and then we blame them and their families for it. It always seemed to me quite pernicious to see intelligence as a fixed quantity.

The next theorist who influenced me was Bourdieu because it fell into place then for me how cultural reproduction actually occured. It is the way in which some families are able to give the things that make education important. Schools should only test things they know the children have experienced and been taught. That perpetuated the whole notion that some children could not actually participate in mainstream education. You had to create a special sub-system.

Also, of course, working with John Rex who was a passionate Weberian

129

I realized that certain groups have vested interests in perpetuating situations. C. Wright Mills influenced me considerably with his notion that private griefs and private problems are, in fact, public griefs and public problems.

This all led to my awareness that there were vested groups in special education. It was full of charismatic figures, and still is, who have their own interests and are dedicated to 'doing good', but their actions do not necessarily 'do good' to groups or to individuals. When this was pointed out, it incurred great hostility from people saying, 'I'm only trying to do good'. OK, I'm not saying you're not trying to do good and you may well be doing good to many children but, as a group, what are you doing?

## Quotations from sample texts

We are sociologists who have an interest in and concern for the policies, practices and individuals in the area of special education. We believe sociological approaches are necessary because the notion that professionals are solely engaged in 'doing good' to weaker groups is not the whole story. Each of the professional groups involved in assessing, referring or teaching have their own vested interests, areas of competence and very real power over their 'clients'. A crucial factor is that these children, adults and parents often have the least say and influence on a number of important decisions on what happens to them and are subject to the most pressure, persuasion and coercion, sometimes quite overt, other times subtle, of any group in the educational system.

Much of what happens in social life is the product of power struggles and vested interests. The task and promise, according to C. W. Mills, is to develop a 'sociological imagination' which makes a distinction between:

> Troubles (which) occur within the character of the individual and within the range of his immediate relations with others; . . .

and

> Issues (which) have to do with matters that transcend these local environments of the individual and the range of his inner life. (C. W. Mills, 1970, pp. 14–15)

This will be a practical tool and will help people to grasp the inter-relationship between history and biography, personal troubles and public issues, including labelling, diagnosis, referral and treatment. These have important relationships to social structures, ideologies and the processes of social and economic reproduction.

Sociological interest in special education will therefore include an analysis of a) the nature and inter-relationship between how categories and classification systems are created, maintained and changed, including the consequences of such events for the participants involved; b) the processes of school life, including interactions between the major participants during their everyday encounters; c) the social construction of knowledge, examining who defines what counts as valuable knowledge and why; d) the relation of special education to the rest of the educational system and the wider society, including the economic and political features of the system.

(1981, p. 18)

In the short term sociology obviously cannot offer any immediate tools for the clinic or classroom, in terms of, say, test procedures or curriculum materials, but even in the short term sociological perspectives should help all students planning to practice in special education.

First, it should help students to question critically the concepts presented to them by other disciplines, and from other viewpoints. For example, much of the descriptive literature on the development of special education asks students to accept that both statutory and non-statutory categories of handicap have gradually evolved, as though spontaneously, over the last hundred years, and that the major problem is matching the categorisations of handicaps, or 'needs', to children. Sociological analysis has begun to show that administrative categories, particularly those that remove children from mainstream education, do not mysteriously develop in an evolutionary manner. Categories appear, change and disappear because of the goals pursued and the decisions made by people who control the special education processes. As a second example, psychological approaches may teach that behaviour modification is a tool for dealing with educationally subnormal children. Sociological perspectives can help students to ask wider social and political questions about the power of some groups to 'modify' the behaviour of other, weaker groups in a society.

(1982, p.22)

What will be the place of those regarded as having special educational needs in economies where levels of education and training are to be raised and national targets met, but only if, individually, young people make greater efforts continually to invest in themselves? It is likely that those designated as 'special' will find it even harder than before to acquire skills and competences that can be exchanged, even intermittently, for work. A majority of them will already, through their previous school career – whether in a segregated or integrated setting – have acquired labels associated with non-competence and, possibly, an identity low in feelings of self-worth. They are likely to suffer more acutely from messages that it is their own responsibility if they fail to acquire the competences necessary to find and keep a job. 'Specials' may find that they have a particular and unenviable place in the political economy of Britain in the new century. The issues go beyond questions of training and employment, however. They are linked to government policies produced to deal with uneconomic citizens.

(1999, p. 246)

## Reflections on inclusive education

In the 1960s, when I was teaching in a primary school in Wolverhampton, many of my class were from Asian and Afro-Caribbean backgrounds and were regarded by the system as 'ESN(M)' (educationally subnormal (moderate) – having moderate learning difficulties) and in need of remedial or special education, although English as a second language was also a factor. It occured to me from that time that it was grossly unfair that children who had just entered a system were regarded as failures in that system and relegated to what I regarded, and still regard, as a non-education. Then I went on to teach in higher education and I focused on the education of 'immigrants' as they called minority ethnic children in the early 1970s. I was concerned that particular groups of children, working-class and immigrant children, were the main ones being relegated to schools for children with learning difficulties and emotional and behavioural difficulties.

I did my PhD on the way in which black children were being placed in ESN(M) schools. I was involved in training teachers to go and work in schools in the Birmingham area where 'minority' children were the majority. That was the first pragmatic influence. I then began to understand the mechanisms by which children were selected out of the education system. It was at a time of the growth of comprehensive schools when they were beginning to question the selection of able children out of the system at the top end but they were sanctioning the selection of the less able out at the bottom end. It is astonishing the number of black adults who have been successful in adult life who have gone through this selecting-out process. In ILEA (Inner London Education Authority) in the 1970s, they were eight times more likely to be placed in special schools. Why it became a political issue, was that they were referred into schools for children with emotional and behavioural difficulty or into Pupil Referral Units.

## Links with different theoretical models

I think I was one of the first to point out that psychological and medical perspectives were the dominant perspectives but to complement this you had to have a sociological perspective. It wasn't a particularly popular view and I did get attacked by a lot of psychologists who felt (a) threatened and (b) that this was removing their rationale for dealing with individual children. I didn't feel that helping children was not a good thing. Most people go into special education with good intentions. We have to face up to the consequences of our actions and the fact that sometimes policies and practices, designed to do good, do exactly the opposite.

I do think that *A Sociology of Special Education* influenced people's thinking. When I did some seminars in the early 1980s, some DfE (Department for Education) officials said to me, 'Yes, we've read your books and we do think there is something we ought to take account of.' I think these perspectives did permeate into civil service thinking. Yet, the dominant theoretical models were still from psychological perspectives. I can understand that the research which has been done by people looking at particular problems, like language delay and communication skills, show how it is important to look at how children develop 'normally' before you look at what goes wrong. Where I challenge this is when people say, 'These children have the problems. We will deal with the child'. They fit the child into the system, rather than saying 'Let's change the system'.

As a sociologist, I am keen to contribute historical theorizing to help our deeper understanding of the development of special educational needs practices. We have continued with an education system in Britain where a superior education is given to elites, so that the state system is neither comprehensive or inclusive. This obsession with selection has persisted and has impeded efforts to create a more inclusive system. It has made me very pessimistic at times that the forces of exclusion are so strong. We've got a narrow, subject-centred, elitist National Curriculum. Pupils who have learning problems have been given the less valued vocational options. We seem to develop subtle ways of excluding.

On the other hand, the development which has made me optimistic over the years is the rise of the disability movement. The way forward is to link people who are excluded with a human rights agenda.

# Profile

## *Klaus Wedell*

### *Professor emeritus, University of London Institute of Education, UK*

## Sample texts

*Orientations in Special Education* (1975)

Special needs education: the next 25 years (1993)

Making inclusive education ordinary (1995)

## Major influences

The major influences on my thinking about inclusion have been the opportunities to see what happens in the real-life situation. These opportunities have come through my practical work in schools from the time of my early research on cerebral palsy, subsequently through my work as an educational psychologist, and through my continuing work in schools during my university work and in retirement. These opportunities have taught me that adults need to be aware of the god-like role they play in deciding the context in which children and young people are expected to develop.

Another set of opportunities came when I visited schools in other countries both in Europe and elsewhere, though my work with the European Community and other agencies. Comparing different education systems showed me how far short these were from achieving the flexibility necessary to respond to individual need if inclusion was to be achieved.

I was also involved in planning groups, such as the Fish Committee (Fish, 1985a), which considered provision for children and young people with special educational needs in the Inner London Educational Authority, and also with the national group which lobbied for adequate special needs legislation after the 1988 and 1993 Education Acts. Although this planning was predicated on the desirability of inclusion, time and again one came up against the rigidities generated by the implementation of policies. The formulation of the Code of Practice was a good example of this. As the result of lobbying the code became a spur for mainstream schools to respond to pupils' individual needs, and yet the procedural overlay often stymies the scope for achieving a flexible response.

## Quotations from sample texts

In recent years there has been an increase in concern for children whose needs are not met in the ordinary school system, and this has resulted in an accelerated expansion of special educational provision. At the same time, a more critical approach to special education has developed. This has probably come about for at least four reasons. Firstly, the outcomes of special educational treatment have often been disappointing. Imposing programmes, often expensive in time, materials and man-power [sic], have sometimes failed to achieve the outcomes claimed for them. Secondly, special education has ceased to be regarded as a charitable gesture made by the non-handicapped members of the community to the handicapped. The recipients of special educational provision, and particularly their families, have become more ready to express their misgivings about shortcomings in the services offered. Thirdly, the current period of economic stringency has made it necessary for administrators to find out whether special educational measures are producing results commensurate with the financial investment made in them. Lastly, along with many other educational principles, the relationship between 'special' and 'normal' education is being re-evaluated.

(1975, p. iv)

Progress in the education of pupils with SENs in the next 25 years will be inextricably linked with developments in educating all children and young people. These developments will start from the recognition that schools cannot meet the diversity of their pupils' needs with the rigidity of preordained classes of standard size, each staffed by a teacher required to provide standard pedagogical approaches to an over-detailed curriculum. Seen from 25 years on, it will seem incredible that we did not use the scope for organisational and pedagogical flexibility which already exists to respond to the particular demands both of the various aspects of a broad and balanced curriculum and of pupils' learning needs. These varied demands call for flexibility in using the range of teacher expertise, non-teaching support, size of pupil grouping, and instructional media including micro-processors. They also call for the participation of pupils, parents and the community, and the involvement of supporting specialist education, health and social services personnel.

(1993, pp. 210–11)

Schools can take ownership of pupil diversity, and be flexible in matching educational approaches to the diversity of *all* pupils' learning needs. The inclusiveness of the education offered would be achieved through the responsiveness offered to *all* pupils. Pupils can be included in tutor groups in secondary schools or in a *home-base* group in a primary school. It is here that the schools' ownership of the diversity of pupils is probably most directly manifested, and where the pupils learn to accept each other as naturally as they would in a family setting. At the same time, inclusion does not necessarily mean that *all* the learning needs of individual pupils will be met by common teaching in groups or even in the *home* school. For *any* pupil, groupings or other arrangements would be determined by his or her learning needs and the demands of the relevant aspect of the curriculum. In such a scenario, inclusion would become the ordinary approach to education, and responding to individual needs would not be regarded as segregation.

As always in a discussion about inclusive education, one will ask whether this degree of flexibility can cover even the most severe levels of SENs. The only answer that one can give is that inevitably the degree of inclusion is determined by the dilemma mentioned earlier: the balance of the realisation of individual abilities against the cost of attempting to achieve it.

(1995, pp. 103–4)

## Reflections on inclusive education

If the fundamental criterion is that the individual needs of children and young people are met, then education systems have to be organized to enable teaching and learning to be facilitated in ways which decouple the attribution of stigma from how pupils are grouped (as I indicate in the article title 'Making inclusive education ordinary'). For example, in the 1960s we set up provision for pre-school and infant aged children with severe language delay and associated problems in a mainstream nursery/infant school. We had a room adjacent to the main hall of the school, where the teacher and speech therapist worked with a group of the children. The door next to the main hall of the school was kept open most of the time, and the children progressively 'included themselves' among the rest of the children, as they became more confident in establishing relationships. The same happened during break times. In this particular instance, the children themselves contributed to decisions about the relative importance of the specific language support they were receiving, and about the benefits of social interaction with the other children in the school.

Although there are many similar examples of piecemeal moves in the direction of inclusion, there would clearly have to be a major shift in education systems if the above criterion was to be achieved. What I have learned, however, is that one would then recognize that the concept of inclusion ceases to be relevant.

## Links with different theoretical models

As far as policy formulation is concerned, probably one of the most important points is to recognize that one often has to live with paradoxes. For example, if you want to meet an individual pupil's needs, you have to identify the pupil. However, with systems as they are, the identification of the pupil is itself likely to interfere with making the provision inclusive. Often people prefer to deny the paradox, and so to align themselves with one or other sides of the dilemma. For example, identifying pupils' individual needs has been associated with 'labelling' children, and so to be eschewed. What is actually required is that the link between identification and the negative attributions of labelling is broken.

The psychological and medical models used in order to understand special educational needs have been given a bad press by some writers. Not only have they been regarded as making invalid assumptions that problems lie 'within' the child or young person, but people using the models have been accused of seeking to promote their own respective professional positions. My own orientation has sometimes been regarded as behaviourist. It seems to me patently obvious that there are no currently developed models which, in themselves, are adequate to explain the complex interactive way in which special educational needs occur. In our area of work, we have to use whatever models – or features of models – appear to offer a hunch to us, the children and their parents – on which to base action. What is crucial is to have an experimental orientation, so that one can progressively eliminate  models which are not making a contribution to a solution. Given the developmental context in which we work, at different stages we may also have to revert to previously discarded models. In this context, being 'eclectic' seems to be the only relevant practical policy.

I have been very taken with the notion of 'compensatory interaction', reflecting ways in which a child's strengths and needs and the resources and deficiencies in the child's environment act on each other in the course of development. This notion has been useful in explaining the fortunate unpredictability of causal relationships in children's development. It also helps to avoid the simplistic views of causation which have bedevilled so many approaches to meeting special educational needs.

# Profile

## *Sheila Wolfendale*
### *University of East London, UK*

### Sample texts

*Assessing Special Educational Needs* (1993)

*Special Needs in the Early Years: Snapshots of Practice* (2000)

### Major influences

When I graduated in Psychology from the University of Hull in 1962, I first taught in a Hull primary school as a class teacher and a remedial teacher. I also worked as an educational psychologist in Hull with John Merritt (who became the Professor of Educational Psychology at the Open University) and then Klaus Wedell. Klaus and I were the only two EPs for the whole city of Hull. It was a steep learning curve in a city where deprivation and need were so prominent.

I think those experiences constituted the major challenge and source of learning. It is the sense you make of those and the constructions you put on them. The experiences themselves were so utterly formative, especially in a city like Hull.

In one of my specialist areas of early identification, there has been an ongoing movement since the early 1970s which has translated into a mandatory procedure for baseline assessment. So baseline assessment in educational legislation has had a long, long gestation before it reached the point of being mandated and there is all sorts of research at a number of levels. I cite baseline assessment as being a major influence because (a) it has been a long-standing issue, (b) it's been an area I have been centrally involved with and (c) it has a bearing on the overall topic of routes to inclusion. I think it is a good example of where research has not yet been shown to be seminal or influential.

## Quotations from sample texts

It is commensurate with an inclusive education approach to regard the reporting requirements and the records of achievement initiatives as being applicable to all children. An entitlement policy demands nothing less than that all opportunities are accessible to all children and their parents.

Within this broad umbrella, certain specific practices have evolved within special needs realms, addressing particular requirements. In fact, as I have noted elsewhere . . . the special educational needs area has been a pace setter regarding parental involvement in assessment. This publication charts the short history in the UK of initiatives exploring the match between professionals' and parents' views, and the use to which data from these sources can be put. Drawing upon a range of parental assessment approaches, a continuum model was posited, which denotes opportunities for parents to write in an open-ended way about their child, towards a 'closed' approach which yields precise information about a child's developmental status, age-appropriate behaviour and skill acquisition.

The Portage check list epitomises the latter approach. *All About Me* – a 'mixed model' – utilises open and closed approaches, and a totally open approach would of course be a diary-like account of events.

The advent of the 1981 Education Act and the opportunity for parents to express their views ('parental advice') as part of the formal assessment process (section 5 of the Act) highlighted the dearth of parental guidance mechanisms to assist them to take up this right. An attempt to redress this was made by this author and other colleagues in a national pilot study, testing out the effectiveness of guidelines to assist parents to write a 'Parental Profile' of their child which could be used as a parental assessment or 'advice' in section 5 assessment.

(1993, pp. 156–7)

The broadest view of inclusion has been expressed thus: it embraces the functioning of families and of societies. In the context of families with disabled children, especially young children, it covers such everyday but important issues as the role of families and friends, and the assistance and support they provide . . .

All models and variations of inclusion have in common a view that parental and child involvement is paramount and a key feature of effective inclusion practice.

(2000, p. 6)

## Reflections on inclusive education

I think the writing on inclusive education, in the last six or so years, has been profoundly influential on people's thinking and the directions of practice. I think the area of early identification has had a percolating effect over the years. I am bound to cite the other area with which I have been centrally involved, which has been bubbling away for years but has

parallels with the legislation. That is parental involvement and special
needs and the fact that successive governments have heeded the call to
involve parents more in their children's education.

If we take an inclusive view of education, it must encompass
the involvement of parents of children with special needs. I think hand
in hand with the evolution of thinking about special educational needs
*per se* is the notion of involving parents to contribute to meeting
their children's needs. That has definitely been part of my development
and has helped to contribute to my changing perspectives. The parental
voice can be very forceful when children can't speak up for themselves
and articulate their needs. Parents who can and do are a force to
be reckoned with and so they help to shape and influence thinking
generally.

As with every innovation, progress is always accompanied by residual
tensions and difficulties. How could it be otherwise if progress is about
changing attitudes? Then it is a question of sometimes lurching forward
and sometimes just progressing in the small, incremental rate. In the last
few years we see there are an increasing number of children with special
needs being included. There are a few LEAs which seem to be pace-setters,
like the London Borough of Newham. The barriers to inclusive education
will only be dismantled progressively over time and progressively
incrementally.

It seems increasingly that the government doesn't mind LEAs being
broken up for different consortia or individuals to take over any part of
the so-called malfunctioning or ineffective LEA. If that is not a recipe for
fragmentation and a loss of collective responsibility for the most
vulnerable children, I don't know what is. I don't know how that ideology
can possibly square with an inclusive approach.

At this point in time, schools are not adequately resourced to take on
all children because the LEAs still retain resources for children with
statements. Unless money going into schools is ring-fenced and
earmarked for special educational needs, I would never be hopeful that it
will be properly allocated and safeguarded.

We need the backing and the inspiration that comes from an ideological
commitment from the top, so to speak. Pro-inclusion people would find
it comforting that we have a government that seems to have gone further
in some ways to promoting the spirit of inclusion, but on the other hand
isn't going anywhere near far enough because it still accepts the notion
that special, separate education is part of the definition of inclusion.

## Links with different theoretical models

We may not have got very far with the notion of the differentiated curriculum ten years on from the Education Reform Act 1988. I don't think
the practice of differentiation is as developed as it could be. Here the

practice is lagging behind the theory. This is all to do with resourcing and expertise.

The theoretical models of psychology used in current training programmes for educational psychologists include ecological and organizational systemic approaches. We take a broader context than before. You get students wanting to come and train as EPs who understand that SEN is not to be narrowly defined. They do understand that schools play a part and have influence in the direction of a child with special needs.

# Overview

The 23 writers whose work has been reflected in Section 2 have spoken for themselves, and continue to do so in the numerous publications which represent their contributions to the field of inclusive ideology and practices.

We said in the preface to our book that these were not the only voices and that, importantly, your own voice is equally important. So, we invite you to conclude your reading of Section 2 in one of two ways, using the methods we adopted in the compilation of this section of the book. Whether or not you have published your own work, you will still have your own ideas, experiences, influences and contributions.

Either ask a colleague to interview you, using some of the key questions given in the preface, ask them then to compile a profile of your career in inclusion to date using the five headings which feature in our 'Profiles' or write your own 1,000–1,500 word 'Reflection' on your own career and contribution to the development of inclusion, to date.

As you move into Section 3, you will see how some of Jenny Corbett's students have made use of the ideas and publications of some of the people featured in Section 2 to develop their own work.

# Section Three

*Linking theory with practice*

Jenny Corbett

# Introduction

This section shows you examples of how other students have related the theoretical debates you have been exploring in Section 1 to their own professional experiences. They may be headteachers, educational psychologists, teachers or learning support assistants. What they all have in common is their need to link theory to practice in their academic writing. One of the aims of this book is to help you to do that.

Section 2 acts as a *bridge* between the theories of Section 1 and the examples of student writing which are discussed in Section 3. It is a *bridge* because it takes a range of contributors to the debates on inclusive education and shows how their professional and personal experiences relate to their theoretical views. It also shows that authors behind the recommended texts on academic courses are human beings like every body else.

From reading Section 2, you may now reflect that:

- it is acceptable to change your theoretical viewpoint as you continue to learn and develop through experience
- to struggle with ambiguity and complexity is a natural process of intellectual growth, not a weakness
- our mind-maps of how we see the world will influence the type of theoretical stance we decide to select from the range available.

If you are able to become more comfortable with using other people's theoretical debates and relating them to your own viewpoint, informed by your professional and personal experience, you are more likely to be able to argue with conviction and clarity. It is this capacity to present your arguments in an analytical structure which illustrates your familiarity and ease with the relevant literature. Debating with a range of viewpoints from published sources in a confident manner is what you are aiming for in your academic writing.

It is useful for you to see examples of how other students argue their viewpoints, using theoretical models. The illustrative extracts selected for inclusion in Section 3 are all examples of excellent writing, in which ideas have been presented with conviction and clarity. Yet the authors are all busy educational professionals like yourselves, fitting in their studies around the rest of their lives. It is important for you to reflect on this.

This book is designed to help you to bridge the gap between seeing those who write the published texts as a very different species from those who write on courses in inclusive education. If you can feel more comfortable around these published authors and their ideas, you can learn to argue with them and to build your own analysis around their various debates.

This section is divided into subheadings which relate to practice rather than to theory. The purpose is to show how pragmatic issues are informed by theory and how theoretical models can help to support the implementation of effective practice. Each subsection concludes with sample questions and tasks which could be used as group activities in teaching sessions and in-service training.

In order that the issues raised can have general application, there is an emphasis on how theory has been linked to practice, rather than upon the detail of the practice itself. There are many ways in which theory can be related to practice. It is not always necessary to do this overtly, using specific references to published texts. The link may be more subtle, illustrating the awareness of different theoretical models and their implications for practice.

## Why relate theory to practice?

This book is entitled 'Theories of Inclusive Education' so why is a section on linking theory to practice considered necessary or appropriate? The subtitle of this book is 'A Students' Guide' and that is why it is necessary to link theory with practice. Theory without practice is arid. Practice without theory is shallow. It is when the two are conjoined that there is creativity, construction and growth.

The examples included in this section show how teachers have digested the theory and reflected on its implications for practice. They illustrate that complex, challenging process of finding ways and means to *realize* ideas and make them work. They do not pretend this is easy or simple. It never is. That is why so many will give up early on, with a despairing cry of 'Unworkable!' Charting that process of struggle and problem-solving is the life-blood of something as difficult as effective inclusive education. Knowing that it is where we want to go does not give us the means to reach it. The territory is always changing, with new demands like the literacy and numeracy strategies having implications for practice. The examples here show that flexibility and responsiveness to change are vital for effective inclusive education to grow and prosper.

For me, making links with these practitioners and their responses to theoretical issues is like closing the circle on my own professional journey. Twenty years ago, I tried to encourage my colleagues in a special school for children with severe learning difficulties to include those children for whom I was responsible who were those with profound and complex disabilities. Within a special school, teachers who were used to working with children who were placed in special provision were still reluctant to include those they saw as 'extra-special'. One of the teachers expressed this as being 'Totally impractical!' At that stage in my career, in the early 1980s, I was in the role of a special school teacher who wanted to extend the daily experiences of the students I worked with and so improve their quality of life. It was very frustrating for me to cope with opposition and resistance to change. Now, as someone who is trying to develop theory which relates to practice, I can see that teachers need to feel empowered to cope effectively. They are inclined to resist if they feel threatened by the process. My current research interest is in learning from teachers working in mainstream schools which are committed to being effectively inclusive. I want to know what they do and say and how they plan to make inclusive education *happen*. It is exciting for me to observe and record the realization of theories of inclusive education. What I am learning is that it is an ongoing process. You don't just *do inclusion* and then that is it. Practitioners have to be constantly responsive, interactive, reflective and willing to adapt. They need to be receptive to learning.

Linking theory to practice is an energizing experience. I have found it exhilarating and uplifting, showing me what can be achieved when teachers and support staff are eager to make it work. It also has to be about sharing community values and having mutual respect between fellow professionals and between teachers and learners. This does not mean it is all sweetness and light. It is a human endeavour and, as such, open to all kinds of tensions and obstacles. An emphasis on community values, which is a fundamental element of inclusive education, means that certain behaviours of individuals who threaten and hurt others have to be confronted. Inclusion does not mean tolerating behaviour which is dangerous. It does mean trying to develop strategies and support systems which help staff to cope and to deal positively with potentially difficult situations. It also means sharing a wider long-term vision which can see people through periods of setbacks and disappointment.

The range of experiences discussed in Section 3 show common concerns which most teachers and support staff will share. These include the following: the challenge of providing a meaningful curriculum for all learners; helping vulnerable learners to feel safe and supported; being receptive to parental anxieties; adapting the Literacy and Numeracy Hours to make them inclusive of all learners; confronting the issue of exclusion in relation to certain learners.

The theoretical debates in Section 1, exploring psychological, sociological, curricular, school effectiveness and disability rights models, will be threaded through Section 3. While headings are going to reflect practice issues rather than theoretical models, they will draw from the various influences. Specific authors which have influenced the student-writer will sometimes be named but are largely left as a composite part of the overall theoretical influence. The headings are in this sequence:

1 Developing an inclusive ethos.
2 Labelling and social exclusion.
3 School effectiveness.
4 Curriculum and pedagogy.

## Developing an inclusive ethos

### *Mainstreaming students with autism or Asperger's syndrome*

Buckton (2000) argues that mainstream education does not always benefit a young person with autism or Asperger's syndrome. He suggests that the difficulties which these young people can have with social understanding will sometimes impede the quality of their mainstream experience. He uses the views of a colleague who has high functioning autism herself to support his argument. She reflects that,

> I have very mixed feelings about mainstreaming. I think it can work well for some autistic spectrum kids and be absolutely disasterous for others. For me, it was pretty bad. I was completely isolated and ostracised . . . My teachers thought I was rude and stubborn and too-clever-by-half . . . I was identified as having special needs . . . and 'behaving just like an autistic child' . . . my major memory of primary school is of spending a huge amount of time being told off and having no idea why, especially as it seemed to happen when I thought I was being most helpful . . . I was an easy target for bullies, especially as the idea of telling anyone just didn't occur to me – I think I just assumed they knew . . . At secondary school I wasn't bullied – just continually aware that no-one liked me, that whenever we were told to pair up in lessons I was always the one left over . . . All in all, it was a major contribution to my developing clinical depression by the age of 13.

The use of this firsthand experience to reflect on the challenges in inclusive education for someone with high functioning autism relates to the concept of 'the personal as political' within the theoretical area of disability studies. There is much evidence from people with a range of different disabilities about the obstacles they encountered in their special schooling experience. There is less available about their difficulties in mainstream. This is an important counterbalance, to reflect that mainstream experience can be particularly challenging for students with autism or Asperger's syndrome. Part of the newly developed 'emancipatory' paradigm in disability research studies is to listen to the voices of disabled people who are recipients of services. Here is a voice which expresses discomfort with the social stigma she experienced in mainstream schooling, although she goes on to say that academically she gained tremendously from the opportunity which led her to university which was 'lifesaving'. Buckton suggests that 'autistic children have difficulty with theory of mind, thus they assume teachers can know what is going on and what they think'. Here, he is drawing from psychological models of children's cognitive reasoning.

Buckton goes on to reflect on those teaching and learning styles which help to connect autistic children into the curriculum, like behaviour modification, facilitated communication and two approaches which have aided communication in his school. One is 'Picture Exchange Communication System (PECS)' and the other is 'Treatment and Education of Autistic and related Communications handicapped Children (TEACCH)' and both draw upon psychological theories of teaching and learning. Several of the theorists in Section 2 say that their main concern is the learners and the extent to which they are fully connected into the learning environment. In this debate on theory and practice, Buckton reflects that for young people with communication difficulties which can often leave them socially isolated and frustrated, it is the *quality* of inclusive education which has to be confronted.

*Task 1: Mainstreaming students with autism or Asperger's syndrome*

Sample questions:

1 Why do you think it is important that the academic area of inclusive education provides a counterbalance to arguments which unreservedly support inclusion into mainstream education?
2 What do you feel is the unique contribution of disabled people who offer evidence of their own experiences of inclusive education?
3 Consider some specialist teaching practices (like TEACCH) which you regard as valuable and reflect on how they support effective learning and whether they can be adopted in a mainstream setting.

*Task:* You are a primary class teacher, asked to include a 7-year-old boy with Asperger's syndrome. What are going to be your main priorities during his first term of inclusion? Think of up to ten key questions you want to ask the specialist support teacher.

## The philosophy, policy and management of inclusion

Pratt (2000) draws her references from a wide net beyond the British context. This helps to give her analysis a social and cultural dimension, in which education is but one reflection of societal value systems. She uses examples from Ireland, Europe and Canada and enters into a dialogue with the views expressed. She quotes Marsha Forest and Jack Pearpoint, two well-known Canadian advocates for inclusive education and talks with them thus:

They said:

Inclusion is about change. Change is terrifying – for all of us – Change upsets us. It's scary. It's unpredictable. But since the issue is one of survival – about the Human Rights of individuals, we must do it anyway. We do not have the right to exclude anyone. Our fears are simply an obstacle to overcome. They cannot and must not be a reason to deny any person their rights.

Put so strongly, inclusion seems the only option! But what is the objective of this inclusion? Certainly not only to have everyone in the one place, belonging. While teaching in a special education class as a trainee, I was surprised to find pupils were amazed to receive praise for their work. One young boy wrote a page about a visit to a pottery. The spelling was appalling and the English a little hard to follow but as he had never written more than a few lines before, I wrote 'excellent' on his work. He came to check with me that I meant it and said he had never had an 'excellent'. He seemed thrilled. For a 12 year old child never to have received such praise supports Susanne Carrington's view that:

this (the British system) was constructed to include some children and not others and in the past this differentiation has meant that some children because of individual deficits 'could not cope' within the ordinary education system (Carrington, 1999).

This lack of tolerance for difference brought about the development of the special education route for those 'not coping'. Perhaps the teachers did not cope with differentiation and felt they should have a group of similar ability to teach. Ballard (1999) suggested that there should be 'an emphasis on diversity rather than assimilation' within a class situation. In an e-mail communication with Matthew Dolmage, from the Coalition for Inclusive Education, he spoke very strongly on the use of special schools:

I don't think any of us can be really effective with inclusion until we get rid of all the other 'places' to which kids/people get sent when the system stops trying. So I would have to say that schools are unlikely to change until special schools no longer exist. Our school system wastes so much energy on assessing, categorising and slotting students that there begins to be an assumption that all kids seen as 'different' are sent somewhere else, which leads to teachers assuming that all the kids left in regular classrooms are 'the same' – a disservice to them too. (Dolmage, 1999)

What is the teaching objective in an inclusive class? I am convinced that it is not to pass exams or to reach level six in Key Stage 3. These may be outcomes of being in the classroom but should not be the objective. There should be no greater thrill for teacher and pupil than to find a pupil understands and uses an idea or concept thought beyond him or her. It makes no difference how simple it seemed to the teacher. It is progress of the best kind.

(Pratt, 2000)

In her analysis, Pratt is drawing from sociological theory, especially that established by Tomlinson. The negative process of schooling for children who consistently fail to achieve is well documented and explored here. In particular, it is her capacity to debate with the ideas in the range of references which marks Pratt's work as both analytically stimulating and stylistically fluent and sharply focused. Quotations are not dropped into the discussion to sink like stones into the bottom of a pond but are caught and bounced as ideas to be examined and extended. References to inclusive education as it is practiced in other countries, drawing extensively from the recent research by Booth and Ainscow, show that subtle differences can be significant. In Norway, Pratt noted that inclusion extended to a whole school policy in which there were long lesson periods, a choice to stay in or go out at break and a free hour of activities each day which were not age specific. Flexibility, at all levels, emerged as a key factor in her comparative study.

Of particular interest to me in her presentation is the use of e-mail debate with authors in the field, some of whom may be communicating exclusively through the Internet. The communication with Matthew Dolmage, of the Coalition for Inclusive Education, illustrates that students now have the facility to enter into a dialogue with those with whose theoretical and ideological debates they engage. The possibilities which this opens up are discussed further in 'Continuing the dialogue' at the end of Section 3.

*Task 2: The philosophy, policy and management of inclusive education*

Sample questions:

1 What are the aspects of inclusive education which make it a philosophical issue rather than only a psychological or sociological dilemma?
2 In what ways can looking at other cultures help us to clarify what we mean by the term 'inclusive education'?
3 Are there practical ways in which mainstream schools can value diverse learning styles within current restrictions and external target-setting?

*Task:* Present the argument for getting rid of all special schooling: present a counter-argument. (This can take the form of a debate if it is done within a group.)

## The reconciliation of policy and practice in inclusive education

Williams (2000) begins her presentation of this issue by defining what 'inclusion' means in a human rights theoretical context. She says:

> The issue of inclusion in education needs to be seen against the background of human rights issues related to the inclusion of all socially disadvantaged groups in mainstream society. It is but one aspect of a broader concern which has dominated the thinking of the 20th century, namely, what is to be considered normal and desirable in any given culture and which members of society should be seen as belonging to the category of 'normal' people.

This introduction immediately links disability rights issues into overall human rights concerns and goes on to discuss social exclusion in its relationship with inclusive education by linking disability rights to discrimination against other minority groups in history. Williams reflects,

' "Inclusion" means inviting those who have been historically locked out to "come in" '.

Having started with a broad contextualizing, she then addressed the practical issues of how schools can be responsive and flexible when there are so many competing demands being made on them. She considers that, 'The present system of children arriving in schools with their support packages tucked under their arms (if not arriving in a wheelbarrow pushed purposefully by their parents), will not work. If inclusion is to be managed successfully, it must be managed holistically'. She explains that this holistic model includes visionary leadership, effective collaboration between all agencies, adequate support for staff and students, parental involvement and effective curriculum planning.

One of the major policy / practice tensions which emerges in her analysis is that between external assessment (e.g. Office for Standards in Education [OFSTED]) and internal prioritizing. This is particularly relevant in the area of teaching approaches, like the balance between whole-class teaching and withdrawal for intensive specialist support. With the Literacy and Numeracy Hours requiring a substantial amount of differentiated whole-class teaching, the use of learning support assistants and specialist teachers to provide additional support, often outside the classroom, is often seen as a key priority in ensuring effective learning.

Williams reflects on the tensions between the OFSTED report and the way in which the primary school she worked in was developing:

> SEN again received a good report and, despite the warnings received about withdrawing children from lessons, this aspect of provision was praised. The inspectors commented that, 'Careful planning with support assistants ensures their time is rigorously spent working in pupils' individual education plans . . . They support pupils in small groups in work areas or in classrooms and give help to individual pupils in particular aspects of their work'. Another section of the report states, 'Pupils with special educational needs are generally given appropriate work to suit their individual needs, and extra help. This is most effectively done when support teachers or assistants take a small group for intensive, well-focused tasks using special resources.' This is a ringing endorsement for a method of delivering teaching which is effectively outlawed by some inclusionist thinking. Comments like this, although flattering in the context of an OFSTED report, send mixed messages to staff who, on the other hand, are being told that 'withdrawal is bad; whole-class differentiated teaching is good'.

This opens up the gap which exists between a theoretically *purist* view of 'inclusionist thinking' and the reality of most teachers' daily practice. Skilled and effective teachers usually use a mixture of methods which, in this instance, may include *some* whole-class teaching and *some* withdrawal for extra support. Some of the theorists (myself included) will be receptive to this degree of flexibility and responsiveness. Others (the 'purists') may not. Williams concludes her analysis with the statement that:

> It is my firm belief that an education system which caters effectively for a wide range of needs and abilities, and thereby allows the majority of children to learn and associate together, holds the best way forward. However, there are pragmatic realities that have to be acknowledged, in order to protect children and teachers from unworkable and unrealistic scenarios.

In this debate, Williams has successfully brought together the broad human rights/disability rights issues with the pragmatics of classroom delivery to show that a realistic and reflective response to practical difficulties is not necessarily negative but can be seen as a first stage to really confronting obstacles and moving forward in a constructive way.

*Task 3: The reconciliation of policy and practice in inclusive education*

Sample questions:

1 What impact does a human rights theoretical perspective have on the issue of inclusive education?
2 Consider arguments for and against the value of withdrawal for intensive support within mainstream provision. Is a mixture of both whole-class differentiated teaching and some individual withdrawal support compatible with an inclusive ideology?
3 What is the role of learning support assistants in the emerging context of Literacy and Numeracy strategies and external assessment procedures?

*Task:* Planning for the most effective use of human resources to support children with Statements of SEN and those on different stages of the Code of Practice:

- what would be your priorities?
- how would you ensure that everyone was working collaboratively?
- how can you effectively share good practice?

Devise a school policy on support systems, considering the range of options and approaches which seem realistic and useful.

## Labelling and social exclusion

### *Gender and special education: what makes boys so 'special'?*

Smith (2000) provides a sociological analysis of why working-class boys are so overrepresented in certain sections of special education, specifically that which caters for those with MLD (moderate learning difficulty) and EBD (emotional and behavioural difficulty). He uses the theoretical model provided by the French sociologist, Bourdieu, to present his analysis. He says that:

Bourdieu argues that the differential educational outcomes/attainments of pupils belonging to different social groups are largely due to the discontinuity between home and school experienced by members of these groups. More widely he emphasises that schools are not culturally neutral and objective institutions but, rather, promote the culture of the dominant classes. He also employs the metaphor of the various forms of capital, in order to show how value may be ascribed to the various cultural forms within society, in order to make the argument as to how cultural differences are interpreted as cultural deficiencies within schools and may thus lead to differential educational attainments relating to the membership of various groups.

Smith did his research in five special schools and three mainstream schools looking at how pupils were being identified and allocated to special schools and at the assumptions, perceptions and understandings of those teachers in special schools who were on the receiving end.

It is unusual for researchers to refer so extensively to Bourdieu in their sociological analysis of the process of exclusion into special schooling through labelling. Foucault is the theorist whose work is most often quoted in this respect. I find it refreshing that Bourdieu is used as the theoretical model as his notion of 'cultural capital', which either advantages or disadvantages individuals in their social status, is highly relevant in the current emphasis on social exclusion and its impact. Smith reflects on his findings by saying that:

> an aspect which was found to be crucial, even decisive sometimes, in determining boys' identifications and allocations to particular 'special' categories such as their lack of conformity to particular forms of bodily control, expression and self management, or their inabilities to produce the 'right bodies' within school were firmly located by teachers within these boys' localities and thereby emanating from their family backgrounds and the kinds of problematic masculinities such backgrounds were believed to produce.

He suggests that it is the process of schooling itself, with the imposed cultural expectations it demands, that makes it incompatible with the inclusion of white, working-class boys. Not only is Smith unusual in using Bourdieu as his template, but his choice of emphasis is also rare, as much recent research has focused upon black, working-class boys. The value of his focus is that it challenges the cultural expectations within our class system, without involving the complex issue of racism. One of the key factors which emerges in his research is a lack of empathy from some teachers who did not value these learners for who and what they were. Smith comments that 'Theirs was not seen as a response to the school at the level of culture, but as a deviant version of a middle class norm'.

As in any qualitative study of this nature, Smith concludes by placing these findings into the broad national context by saying that:

> The educational politics of recent years have constructed issues relating to pupils' membership of wider groups and location within society as irrelevant

or, at most, peripheral to their performance within schools. An attempt has been made to remove such considerations from educational debates and to replace them with a narrow, mechanistic view of education, one which ignores the social, economic and cultural complexities of schools and the communities they serve. Moreover, the accompanying legislation of these years has also had the effect of magnifying the consequences of the unequal social power whose relevance such an approach denies! This has led almost inevitably to a further disadvantaging of those pupils most at risk of being processed as having SEN.

This kind of research is valuable in the debates on inclusive education as it forces us to see schooling in its wider social context and to reflect upon the effect of increased gaps between the haves and have nots. Where some mainstream schools are now taking up to 50 per cent of pupils with special educational needs, within the Code of Practice, there is a real question arising as to where the boundaries exist between schools that are becoming increasingly exclusive and those which are becoming more inclusive. Mainstream no longer necessarily means inclusive. It can just mean another kind of 'special', potentially without sufficient resources.

*Task 4: Gender and special education – what makes boys so 'special'?*

Sample questions:

1  How can reference to the ideas of a sociological theorist like Bourdieu contribute to the debates on inclusive education and the impact of exclusion?
2  Does schooling only involve teaching and assessment or does it need to recognize and be sensitive towards the social, economic and cultural complexities of its community?
3  How does this concern with white working-class boys in special education link into current political debates on social exclusion?

*Task:* Consider the various ways in which education uses a middle class norm by which to judge individual effectiveness. What approaches can help schools to show respect for differences? Are there ways in which teachers can be taught to be more empathetic? Consider some ways which could be usefully applied in schools.

## Emotional and behavioural difficulties and social exclusion

Spiers (2000) links the issue of exclusions from school, on the grounds of difficult behaviour, to the current emphasis on social exclusion. She draws from a published government document (Sparkes, 1999) to reflect that there now seems to be national concern expressed for those young people who are not included in schooling or society. She then directly links theory and practice by suggesting that a difference persists 'in the perceptions of the practitioners (teachers and headteachers) and those outside school, with regard to dealing with challenging behaviour'. She reflects that:

> I suspect that the majority of teachers, rather than feeling themselves to be
> 'reflective practitioners', feel themselves besieged, trying to cope with extremely
> challenging behaviour in their classrooms in a context where the government
> is telling them to reduce the numbers of permanent exclusions. Without an
> attempt to bridge the gap between these perceptions, schools may continue to
> find ways of excluding students. Do we fully recognise the contradictions and
> dilemmas posed by the values of equality and fairness than underpin the argu-
> ments for inclusion?

I think this is a very good question to ask, because it is both thoughtful
and powerful. Here is an example of a reflective practitioner in the most
pertinent sense who is asking for a careful consideration of the practical
consequences of theoretical ideology.

Spiers refers to the notion of a 'post-positivist model' which Clarke,
Dyson and Millward (1998) say is one which relies on analysis, critique
and a deconstruction of existing concepts, and which is part of the relatively unchallenged, liberal approach in current theorising. Spiers, in her
analysis, decides to 'consider some flaws of the post-positivist model in
the debate over permanent exclusions'. She then uses an example:

> In a lesson recently, I witnessed Pupil A interacting in a very negative way with
> another student, Pupil B. Pupil B is a physically disabled pupil with a state-
> ment, who the school has tried hard to include. Despite my best efforts as an
> experienced and generally successful teacher, I found it very difficult to prevent
> Pupil A behaving in a detrimental and aggressive way to Pupil B. For me, this
> highlighted the principles of equality of opportunity and fairness in an uncom-
> fortable way. It made me realise the relative nature of concepts like equality and
> fairness. In offering Pupil A equality and fairness, are we depriving other stu-
> dents of them? Is it right in the case of Pupil A to assume that 'inclusion' in a
> mainstream school is *a priori* beneficial to either him or other students? All the
> evidence, albeit anecdotal, is to the contrary.

Spiers goes on to suggest that 'we have to accept that we have social
mores, conventions and standards which are embodied by our social institutions including our schools'. It is interesting to compare her analysis
with that provided by Smith in the earlier example. He seemed eager to
challenge these social mores in order to foster more inclusive attitudes.
You may want to consider which view you feel more in sympathy with,
and why.

As the wide range of perspectives in Section 2 of this book illustrates,
there are many different and sometimes contrasting ways to present views
on inclusive education. There are no right ways and no wrong ways, as
far as I am concerned anyway, although the purists may not countenance
any view other than their own. As long as you can justify the approach
you are taking (as Spiers skilfully does in this instance) you have every
right to express a view of your own. Where this is fuelled entirely by

personal prejudice and your own experience and feeling, minus a careful consideration of the expression of other views, then this approach is unlikely to gain much academic credence.

Hall (2000) suggests that there may be ways in which schools can become more inclusive of all learners. He presents a very cohesive and carefully thought through evaluation of how theory can be converted into effective practice:

> One controversial step that I would propose is to widen the scope of individual education plans to include all pupils of statutory school age (a policy implied in a recent speech by David Blunkett). The aim of this would be to try to take away the SEN label and thus de-stigmatise a large portion of special education provision. This would also involve the de-structuring of current 'SEN' systems and the forming of a new 'pupil welfare' department which *every* pupil would be served by, hopefully aiding quick identification of problems and solutions. This would provide a much more proactive model.
>
> The presence of trained specialists on site or, at most, resident between two or three schools, would concentrate the expertise at the grass roots level rather than having 'consultants' (educational psychologists, counsellors etc.) floating in and out and leaving much of the provision in the hands of untrained, low paid 'carers'. This would lead to a much more cohesive approach, a wide variety of interventions, and access to these as the need arose.

This analysis shows how theory and practice are inextricably interwoven: finding a problem-solving approach to current flaws addresses weaknesses in the theorizing at the same time as illustrating current practice limitations.

Hall proceeds to examine a recent government report in relation to his own practice, by saying that:

> A recent report commissioned by the DfEE concerning EBD [emotional and behavioural difficulties] in mainstream schools (DfEE, 1999) found that effective practice was characterised by the following:
>
> * good general teaching
> * an appropriate curriculum
> * an effective behavioural policy
> * effective leadership from senior management
> * the presence of key members of staff who understand the nature of EBD
>
> From my own experience I would add that, as more and more pupils come into schools needing extra help regarding EBD issues, the pressure for examining the school's fundamental role increases. Schools, for a variety of reasons, are reluctant to diminish their academic role. In my view there needs to be a change in their perspective such that they begin to embrace the fact that they must become a centre for 'learning' – academic, social and emotional. By doing this, they would open themselves up to becoming a community with on-site provisions for many types of beneficial interventions for pupils in need and thus work in a more practical way to provide 'Equality of Opportunity' and excellence for all.

In summary, my view is that the system is still being continuously 'tweaked' and prodded in the hope of producing an effective model for inclusion and while current proposals are encouraging, I feel that they are not far reaching enough and need to adopt a much more holistic approach.

Hall offers an excellent example of thoughtful analysis which relates theory and government directives to what he and his colleagues are experiencing in the workplace. His call for a holistic approach is redolent of Smith's earlier critique of the lack of empathy and understanding among some teachers.

These are practitioners who have much wisdom and insight to share with theorists. They are problem-solvers who are willing to try out strategies but want to know what they are supposed to do when some methods clearly do not work effectively. Theorists must listen to practitioners if they are to avoid a descent into that theoretical desert so regretted by Clarke, Dyson and Millward (1998) in their analysis.

*Task 5: Emotional and behavioural difficulties and social exclusion*

Sample questions:

1 Why are there evident tensions between the need for schools to demonstrate high academic achievement and the inclusion of students with emotional and behavioural difficulties?
2 In what practical ways can schools become more holistic and empathetic in their responses to learners who bring a range of emotional difficulties to school from their wider social experiences?
3 To what extent can whole-school policies on behaviour help schools to cope more effectively with learners who are disruptive to others?

*Task:* Debate the following topic, with speakers for and against: some students will always have to be excluded for the well-being of the majority.

## Inclusion and school effectiveness

### Inclusion: raising standards for all

Mansaray (2000) uses a wide range of relevant references to discuss this issue, which include recent articles from the *Times Educational Supplement* (*TES*) as well as academic books and papers. This is a useful way to approach any literature review in education, as the weekly newspaper provides up-to-date information and analysis which other sources lack. She says, for example, that:

> An article in the *TES* (October 1, 1999), for instance, asserted that 'measures to raise educational standards and the drive to enrol more children with special needs in mainstream schools are cancelling each other out'. Interestingly, LEAs like Newham, which have adopted a very strong inclusive education policy,

actually challenge this orthodoxy as their results improve year on year. A more recent article in the *TES* (December 3, 1999) shows deprived authorities whose schools include very diverse pupil populations doing much better than wealthier ones. In the top 25% of councils were Tower Hamlets and Newham.

From my own experience, I saw an inclusive approach work to the benefit of all pupils. From 1992 to 1998, I was learning support coordinator in a girls' comprehensive school where the English department moved to having fully inclusive mixed-attainment groups. With my team, I had already introduced a partnership teaching approach in the school. We would plan and team teach alongside mainstream colleagues in order to make the curriculum accessible to all pupils, including those with statements. The result in the English department was a dramatic improvement in English GCSE results, which was maintained year on year. This despite the large numbers who, on entry to Year 8, had reading ages below nine years and many well below eight years.

We need more teachers and education professionals who are ready to say that inclusion which works raises standards for all. A link which this government have made in their 'Programme of Action' (DfEE, 1998) is when they say that 'An increasing number of schools are showing that an inclusive approach can reinforce a commitment to higher standards of achievement for all children.' (p. 23). Ainscow's (1998) work on linking school effectiveness and inclusion is I think very helpful in this regard, in particular the development with Booth and CSIE (Centre for Studies on Inclusive Education) of an Index of Inclusive Schooling.

In this sequence, Mansaray has threaded theoretical influences into examples of practice in a way which serves to heighten the connectedness.

She demonstrates a real capacity to express her own views alongside an analysis of the perspectives drawn from recent literature when she says:

> I firmly believe we need to read educators like hooks and Paolo Freire to free us from our current obsession with the academic outcomes of schooling. Children are no longer human beings but level 2s or 4s or As to Cs! As teachers we have been recruited to a 'Gradgrind' view of education where children are empty vessels ready to be filled with digraphs or number bonds! Where is education as preparation for life and living? At times it certainly feels like we are experiencing hard times.

I don't feel this could be expressed better by any of the theorists. It shows a 'thinking' and a 'feeling' reflective practitioner, who is challenging existing developments, from a sound base of evidence and wide reading.

### Task 6: Inclusion – raising standards for all

Sample questions:

1  Which aspects of supportive and collaborative practice help to make an inclusive school one that is also an effective school?
2  This author was looking at 'new ways of seeing old connections'. How might an open approach to new ways of 'seeing' help schools to move

forward into a more proactive approach to demonstrating ways of being effective?

3  Should a commitment to inclusive education necessitate a re-evaluation of priorities within the existing mainstream curriculum?

Task: Find examples from weekly journals like the *Times Educational Supplement* which reinforce or challenge the bond between inclusion and schools which demonstrate effectiveness. From this process, assess the key characteristics of an 'effective inclusive' school.

## School effectiveness: a comparison between two schools

Fasan (2000) suggests that inclusion is only worthwhile if a school is demonstrably effective. Two schools are compared for their effectiveness:

> Looking at School 'E', the school rules and policies were clearly structured and set out, such that the children knew what was expected of them, and there were consequences for non-compliance. However, in School 'O', notwithstanding that there were school rules, the children did not adhere to them because sanctions were not always carried out. Besides, there were many children with challenging behaviour and the school could not formulate effective strategies to deal with the situation. Lack of control was evident in the classroom and in the whole school system. Moreover, the children appeared to be more interested in being disruptive than in learning. In effect, the whole purpose of inclusion was being hampered.

What Fasan has usefully raised here is the vexed question of 'Exactly what kind of schooling experience are these learners being included within?' It is very important to ask this question, as there is severe criticism of the quality of much which passes for mainstream state education, especially at the secondary school stage. If a school is poorly managed and out of control and there is a general ethos of anti-learning, then this is clearly not an environment which supports effective inclusion. Inclusion has to be into something worth having, a quality experience which is generally attractive to other consumers.

The comparisons continue:

> In school 'E' most of the teachers and pupils were proud of the school and their departments. They were involved in other school issues and most of the staff have held their position for some time. This enabled them to review progress over the years and develop new strategies. There was also a lot of collaborative work going on.
>
> In school 'O', there was a cloud of general tension, stress and unsettlement which stemmed from all kinds of pressure, generated from inside and outside the school. The senior management of the school was under a lot of pressure to meet OFSTED's requirements and come off special measures. The teachers seemed exhausted and stressed and did not have a good working relationship

with the senior management. Hence, this resulted in high staff turnover and long-term sickness absences.

As Fasan goes on to emphasize, the evidence of significant differences in achievement between schools in similar catchment areas points to the importance of good management.

Reflections on the role of parents in developing an effective school community is something which is not always discussed in detail but Fasan views this as crucial:

> There are a lot of vulnerable children who do not have proactive parents that can advocate on their behalf with the school. In school 'E', for instance, there was an active PTA with strong views about education. They organised meetings and responded to situations within the school. Parents in school 'O' generally seemed to be interested in their individual children, while some did not keep track with their children's performance.
>
> Also, there was not a Parents' Association or a strong group of similar standing that could come together to make decisions. The few parents involved in the school were the Parent Governors. There appeared to be an under-representation of parents. A lot of parents felt helpless and had to depend on the school as a last resport to have a say in their children's behaviour and education.
>
> The resultant effect of this is that most children with learning difficulties are from poor, working-class backgrounds, and they are more likely to be educated in the same low status schools (Slee *et al.*, 1997). On the other hand, the middle-class parents understand the school system and because they have a stronger say, they are able to influence their children's education. It is significant that parents have a strong voice within the school. This enables them to get more involved in their children's education and to give their views and support towards the school's progress. This would, in turn, foster a sense of commitment by parents and all other educators and the children.

This emphasis links back to the issues raised by Smith in relation to Bourdieu's 'cultural capital'. Parents are becoming an increasingly influential force in education and they are highly instrumental in the effectiveness of a school. Inclusive education has to mean inclusion into a school which most parents value and support and not into a school which parents only opt for because it is the only one which will take their child.

*Task 7: School effectiveness – a comparison between two schools*

Sample questions:

1 Why can school effectiveness be viewed as an aspect of equality of opportunity?
2 What are the major tensions between being a demonstrably effective school and an inclusive school?
3 Where are the main challenges for effective inclusive education in relation to parental expectations?

*Task:* Draw up a list of features of an effectively inclusive institution. Look at a school or college you know well. Is it both effective and inclusive? In what ways is it so? If it is not so, how is this shown?

## Curriculum and pedagogy

### *The Literacy Hour*

The impact of the Literacy Hour on teaching methods in primary class-rooms in England and Wales has been dramatic and has significant implications for children with learning or behavioural difficulties. Teachers have been observing and recording the ways in which children are responding.

Bryan (2000) observed the responses of several children with emotional and behavioural difficulties. She felt that:

> There was a great deal of very effective, inclusive teaching going on. The strategies teachers used were those that would be considered 'good practice' in any classroom. What I noticed was that these strategies were often exaggerated, for example, praising a child more frequently than appeared necessary when they remained on task. The strategy worked well with that group of children. The children smiled a great deal and remained on task, completing the work to the high standard set by the teacher. The teachers also used their relationship with, and knowledge of, the children to praise the efforts of individuals and make comments personal. It was very positive to see how well teachers anticipated potential problems and either calmed a child or diverted their attention so that the child could return to work in the right frame of mind.
>
> The problems seemed to come if the teachers were inconsistent in any area of their classroom management. For example, a child who essentially opted out of the lesson did so because the teacher did not reinforce the acceptable code of conduct from the start and later challenged the child's behaviour. Once the child had been allowed to exploit the code of conduct, it became more and more difficult for the teacher to focus the child again and a confrontation between teacher and child was inevitable.

Her reflections reinforce the theorizing on pedagogy which has long favoured 'good quality teaching for all'. In all the early 1980s emphasis upon the importance of integration for children with disabilities and learning difficulties, which followed on from the publication of the Warnock Report in 1978 (DES, 1978), there was an implication that integration of itself was the major issue. Hegarty, and many other theorists since, have insisted that it is 'good teaching' which children with special educational needs want, not just integration. As Fasan's research illustrated, inclusion into a mainstream school in which teaching is inadequate and management is ineffective is not an acceptable deal for any children.

Beattie (2000) was addressing three issues in her research which were:

- the problems or benefits the Literacy Hour creates for the child with ADHD (Attention Deficit Hyperactivity Disorder)
- how far the literacy hour meets the needs of the child
- what variables affect the above.

She examines different stages of the Literacy Hour in detail:

The first fifteen minutes of the hour are spent on shared reading and/or shared writing. Many teachers have welcomed this more than any other sector (Lewis and Fisher, 1999). However, the success of shared reading can depend on the use of appropriate and quality literature. It is not clear how this quality is being interpreted and by whom (Dadds, 1999). The experience can be advantageous and/or problematic for the child with ADHD. The novelty of large print and pictures in a big book can promote interest and therefore sustain concentration. The repetition of using the same text over several days, and then a similar format every week, provides the consistency needed for the ADHD child (Munden and Arcelus, 1999), but the novelty factor is lost and concentration subsequently may decrease.

She goes on to examine the stage of 'focused word and sentence work':

These children are often very creative. The focused skills approach can minimise the creative and maximise the stultifying. This section does however lend itself to short, fun activities and an abundance of pupil participation, the dynamics of which can keep the interest of the ADHD child. There is, subsequently, a particular requirement here to wait turns appropriately . . . The child with ADHD may blurt out answers before the question is finished, or interrupt others because of difficulty in awaiting turn, and this disrupts the pattern of thinking for all involved. By the end of these two sessions, the class has usually been required to sit for thirty minutes. This is very demanding on the hyperactive nature of the ADHD child.

Beattie then looks at the plenary section of the Literacy Hour:

The plenary requires a listening culture 'to enable pupils to reflect upon what they have learned . . . develop an atmosphere of constructive criticism' (DfEE, 1998, p. 13). Although only ten minutes long, their short attention span has struggled with fifty minutes of literacy prior to this, and so to be an active volunteer and listener at this point is a tough demand.

Finally, she explores the value of group work within the Literacy Hour:

This is a situation the child needs and suffers from a lack of in the whole class teaching sessions. Feedback is immediate and can be made personally relevant. Concentration during the one to one contact time is therefore at an optimum and this is a useful time to help them learn independent reading/writing strategies successfully. It is vital that ADHD is tracked regularly. Close observation gives teachers reliable information on progress, exploiting any concerns, emotional or academic.

The more informal setting of group work could however give rise to the lack of self discipline contained in the disorder. Also it would seem that a situation where children are reading out loud at different paces is potentially very distracting, especially for a child who has difficulties with sustaining attention when there is any other noise or movement. However, from my experience with ADHD children, if the interest level is high with the text and the teacher in close vicinity, they cope remarkably well. This highlights the importance of these two factors.

In her concluding analysis, Beattie addresses the key variable as she sees it which is 'the teacher' and the qualities brought to that role. It is the specific skills deployed by the mainstream class teacher and support staff which make all the difference between a child with ADHD being able to cope effectively or being potentially excluded. She reflects that:

> Social approval/disapproval is best given when the child is working independently and where co-operation is required, such as discussing the text in guided reading group sessions, and sharing ideas in the plenary.
>
> Teachers need to address a balance between what to ignore and what to feed back on. They are then in control of the situation, rather than being controlled by the child. The child then starts to realise at what parts of the hour attention can be gained and at what parts it is more problematic. It can be questioned here that those working with ADHD individuals are faced with a conflict. How far have the children got a right to 'live' their disorder? Should we as professionals always try to correct their deficits with different approaches and feed back, or ignore the behaviours?

I find Beattie's analysis fascinating throughout. She goes into great detail about the nature of ADHD and the ways in which a modified pedagogy can help to effectively include these children. In so doing, she draws extensively on psychological theoretical models of individual child-deficit. Although this approach has fallen out of favour among many sociological and disability studies theorists, it is one with which most teachers in schools are familiar. If the curriculum and teaching approaches are to be investigated in detail to see how they can accommodate a diverse range of learning styles, this may necessitate an assessment of how different children learn best and what strategies can support their learning. This means recognizing that they have specific problems and confronting these as their individual needs.

These kinds of debates are to be found in school staffrooms throughout the world. It is the very foundation of teaching as a professional skill that pedagogy and the curriculum has to be appropriate for the needs of the learners. Perhaps this is one of the sensitive areas of tension between some teachers working at the grass roots and some theorists working in academia. The teachers have to produce a *workable* structure to get them through each day in the classroom, operating in a dynamic, unpredictable, interactive process. Academics have the luxury of detachment, where they can examine the concepts, vocabulary and broad picture without having to be confronted with the detailed reality. Where the two groups can work collaboratively (for example, in much of the current work being developed by theorists like Ainscow and Booth), there is more likely to be a useful bridge built which can foster productive sharing of perceptions.

*Task 8: The Literacy Hour*

Sample questions:

1 In what ways is the Literacy Hour potentially inclusive in its long-term benefits and in what ways is it excluding?
2 Are there some strategies which teachers have developed to help children with difficulties like those caused by Attention Deficit Hyperactivity Disorder which might be usefully applied to other children within an average mainstream classroom?
3 What aspects of pedagogy would you say are 'specialist' in relation to EBD or ADHD and which can be used by any skilled teacher or learning support assistant?

*Task:* Prepare a framework of teaching skills and materials required to present an effective Literacy Hour session for a particular group of learners with whom you are familiar.

## Curriculum and pedagogy for diversity

One of the central features of inclusive education is that it is about teaching for diversity. In this process the teacher has to be flexible and adaptive, recognizing that different learners have varied ways of interpreting and understanding information. Developing an inclusive pedagogy in mainstream schooling means learning to be adaptable and imaginative in approach.

Purdie (2000) reflects on the role of learning support assistants (LSAs) in supporting children with speech and language difficulties in the Literacy Hour:

> I support assistants in two separate schools in implementing a programme for teaching phonological awareness. In one school this is seen as a facility for a group of children who are included in it alongside the target child; in the other school a narrower view of support is taken and it is carried out individually with the child. The former seems to me to better support an inclusive approach to education.

Purdie notes that children with speech and language difficulties often have significant difficulties with phonological awareness and they benefit from a whole-school policy on structuring the learning of phonics. Her reflections draw from a psychological model of children's cognitive development but they are also grounded in school effectiveness, curriculum and pedagogy. What is particularly interesting to me is that her suggestions seem to reiterate what has long been standard wisdom in relation to inclusive education: *teaching approaches which are valuable for children with special needs are often valuable for all learners*. This is important to consider. If we believe that what works effectively with those who experience difficulties for a range of reasons is also useful to others, we are merging the mainstream and special. Surely, the pedagogy and curriculum which is seen as responsive to individual needs is that which is to be preferred.

Mizon (2000) reinforces the importance of a merging between what is seen as special and mainstream practice, in her focus on a boy with a statement relating to his learning difficulties and visual impairment. In this example, the mainstream teacher felt overwhelmed by his visual impairment and this became a real obstacle in his full inclusion in the curriculum. Mizon says that:

> I felt a plan of action needed to be implemented if the situation was to be salvaged. The peripatetic teacher came in and spent a morning observing the teacher and Sam. This was quickly followed by another period of observation. Then a planning meeting between myself, the class teacher, the peripatetic teacher, Sam's LSA and the LSA attached to the VI (Visually Impaired) base was arranged. The peripatetic teacher discussed her observations with the group and offered ways to move forward. She also pointed out the many examples of good practice that she had observed, thus raising the teacher's self-confidence. Discussing the issues and finding workable strategies helped the teacher to feel empowered and in control. Thus the 'specialist' is facilitating acceptance, inclusion and good practice.

This focus on empowering the mainstream teacher is a vital element in creating an inclusive pedagogy and an aspect which is reinforced by many theorists.

However, issues are not always resolved as easily as in Mizon's example. Sometimes, it is quite evident that children are being excluded by the curriculum and pedagogy. Burgess (2000) offers an example of a girl with learning and behavioural difficulties who is a passive participant:

> Initially J. is quiet and keeps her head down, arms round her work to keep prying eyes away, pretending to answer the questions. After about twenty minutes, however, she starts to fiddle around with some pencils and rulers on the table and begins to pull the table towards herself and back again. The teacher keeps reprimanding her until she loses two minutes of play. The maths test is far too complicated for her ability and her answers bear no relevance to the questions asked. She was quite happy to 'blend in' at first but now looks bored and restless. Two of the boys sitting at the far end of J.'s table catch on to the fact that she hasn't written anything and start to comment. 'Hey, miss, look she hasn't even written her poem yet. She's really thick. Der brain.' The teacher is over the other side of the classroom and, due to the noise level, hears none of this and therefore does nothing to stop it. J. is used to this type of abuse and ignores it.

Burgess links this observation of practice directly into theoretical debates:

> Corbett and Norwich (1999) tell us that it is a connective pedagogy which promotes an inclusive school community and an inclusive pedagogy relates to how

much of the time the individual learner is being connected into the learning environment. We can therefore say that the main pedagogies used on that day of whole class teaching and lack of differentiated work were quite unsuitable for J. as she was unable to join in the maths test or attempt to write a poem. The pedagogies used did not allow her to access the learning environment which also meant she was excluded from the classroom culture.

In her analysis, Burgess is doing what I suggested at the beginning of Section 3 was the hallmark of good quality academic writing. She links her own research findings directly to theoretical arguments, building from these to add a further dimension. As I shall indicate in the concluding 'Continuing the dialogue' discussion, it is the rapport between theorists and practitioners which forms the creative growth of <i>lived theory</i>.

In some examples of effective pedagogy, it may be that the teacher is working in a segregated, special school environment but feels they are being <i>pedagogically inclusive</i> in that they are making available to their pupils a breadth of curriculum previously denied to them.

Santi (2000), for example, reflects on her teaching experience in a special school for children with severe learning difficulties (SLD) and profound and multiple disabilities (PMLD). She decided to work with her group for a 20-minute oral session focusing on numbers between 1 to 10, as part of the Numeracy Strategy. She says that:

> My class is a Year 6 class that consists of 4 verbal SLD pupils, 1 non-verbal pupil and 2 PMLD pupils. My hardest task was to plan a lesson that each of my pupils could be involved in, this being such a mixed ability class. For my planning I referred to the Reception syllabus. To meet the needs of the PMLD pupils I had to find stages in developmental maths that tied in with the focus of the lesson. The oral session included a lot of counting out loud for the verbal pupils and using very tactile objects and Velcro counters for the less able pupils, in order for them to experience the existence of objects as a number. The oral lesson went well and pupils were able to take part at their own level. A very positive outcome from this was a real sense of togetherness that was created within the group and the pupils interacted extremely well, which is something that some SLD and PMLD pupils find hard to do naturally.

Here is a young teacher reflecting on how she can make these sessions meaningful for all the wide range of learners she has in her group. It is rather poignant as an example of an inclusive pedagogy for me, for it takes me back to that stage of my own teaching career when my special school colleagues were unwilling to include 'my' children, who were learners with profound and multiple disabilities (PMLD), in their teaching sessions. For these reasons, because attitudes have become more inclusive and flexible at all levels, it is important to recognize that this is an example of inclusive pedagogy and not just segregated provision.

Santi (2000) goes on to suggest that:

> There are many positive aspects that can be pulled out from the Numeracy Strategy and lessons can work well. The structure of the hour is easy to imple-

ment but the content does not lend itself to the majority of the pupils' needs. For example, the PMLD groups are excluded from much of the content. Similarly, Key Stage 1 pupils become excluded.

Despite these reservations, she looks positively at an inclusive curriculum and the potential it has for increasing experiences for all learners:

> We need to look at the Numeracy Strategy as a benefit to special schooling and not just a mere attempt to include all pupils. If the Numeracy Strategy is going to be taught within special schools, then I think the curriculum needs to be revised so that it is appropriate and useful to the pupil's needs. Much work needs to be focused in special schools on all the areas that mainstream pupils are naturally expected to know. Pupils with SLD and PMLD must learn in all aspects of their lives. They must learn to shop, recognise money, tell the time, recognise bus numbers – the list goes on and on. The mathematics that they learn needs to be practical and helpful to their needs. We must provide them with all the skills so that they may be as independent as possible later on in their lives. The Numeracy Strategy content as it stands at present does not lend itself to this.

It is important to include this voice from the special school context within a comprehensive discussion of linking inclusive education theory into practice. Some learners, particularly those with profound and multiple disabilities, are still within the segregated sector. Santi gives us an awareness of how general curriculum initiatives can have broader application which extends and enriches the learning experience of those she teaches. The same skills of effective *inclusive pedagogy* which apply in mainstream schooling are relevant in this context: flexibility; adaptability; understanding of individual differences; respect for different learning styles. Santi is drawing from either ends of the theoretical spectrum, in her use of psychological models of individual need and her concern for the human rights of young people with the most profound disabilites. These are the group who are often marginalized within the disability movement, as they are unlikely to speak up for their rights. Santi shows that part of her role as teacher is to protect their interests to ensure they are not excluded from potential stimulus within new curriculum initiatives.

### Task 9: Curriculum and pedagogy for diversity

Sample questions:

1  In what ways can a merging of specialist and mainstream pedagogies enrich the learning experiences of all learners?
2  How can specialist teachers help to empower mainstream teachers to feel confident in their teaching approaches?
3  What aspects of bringing an inclusive pedagogy into special education settings can be seen to be enriching and innovative?

*Task:* Consider what an inclusive pedagogy means in practice. What particular examples of practice would you put forward as being valuable for all learners? Are there any specific ways in which the curriculum can be adapted to be more inclusive? Collate examples of good practice and decide why they are 'good practice'.

# Continuing the dialogue

## Jenny Corbett

Students are now using the Internet and e-mail to do their research. This is a relatively recent development and one that has profound implications for any form of higher education studies. Compared to when I was doing my PhD research, when a letter to a key academic other than my supervisor was probably the nearest I got to a long-distance dialogue, students now have the opportunity to engage in genuine dialogue with a diverse range of thinkers.

This opens up the following possibilities:

- issues which are difficult to conceptualize can be clarified through an e-mail debate between academic writers and students
- ideas being generated from the global arena are available to take students beyond national boundaries
- students may have access to texts which are in the process of being created, long before they actually get published, and while the writer is still receptive to dialogue and suggestions.

For an academic area like inclusive education, this use of new technological advances has the potential to encourage the evolution of an inclusive educational process in action. It is the opening-out and breaking of barriers which can help to make this happen.

In recent years, for example, there has been a significant expansion of disabled students coming into a wide range of courses in higher education, particularly in America, Australia and Britain. As was evident in the debate in Section 1, there has also been a growth in the establishment of new departments or centres of disability studies in universities, in which many of the key academics are themselves disabled. The use of the Internet and e-mail effectively opens up access to learning in higher education if it continues to develop at its current rapid rate. Physical boundaries are no longer the major issue they once were. New technology also enables students whose difficulties with writing, spelling and grammar would have prevented their participation in higher education in the mid-twentieth century, to be properly included through twenty-first century tools of communication.

In an academic discourse of 'Inclusive Education', it is this new potential for a genuine dialogue which really excites me. It will mean a reframing of what we mean by academe. For this dialogue to work effectively, to be really inclusive, requires a realignment of power differentials. The academic has to let go of being 'the expert'. The student gains the power of being in a position to properly influence the growth of theory through creative dialogue. Academics will be able to listen, through e-mail, to disabled people telling them about their experiences and perceptions, responding directly to the ideas being generated about 'inclusive education'. Teachers, working in schools and colleges, will be able to make valuable contributions to the growth of new theories on effective inclusive education and what strategies for success can be usefully shared. This is already happening through professional e-mail support networks. In Britain, for example, it is through initiatives like 'The SENCO (Special Educational Needs Co-ordinator) Forum', in which teachers can share their challenges and ways of coping with difficulties as they arise. The next step is to foster dialogue between these professional networkers and those who develop theories, so that they can learn from one another.

I see this as the most positive way forward and a path which leads us away from the destructive 'navel-gazing' which Clark, Dyson and Millward (1998) felt uneasy with as a model of theorizing special education. This form of genuine dialogue, which is about listening, sharing, reflecting, arguing and developing ideas, is the most creative and forceful way in which theories on inclusive education can be generated to make them realizable as ways of creating effective practice for the twenty-first century. If we want to avoid atrophy in theorizing in inclusive education, we need to be open to learn from those who experience it and those who do it. Disabled students and teachers should be part of the theorizing if they are to be fully supported in undertaking what is a challenging process of growth and collaborative development.

# Bibliography

Aaron, J. (1997) Crip pride, poem in *Cripzine: Disability Arts and Culture*. Website http://www.stanford.edu/-jarron/crip.htm

Ainscow, M. (ed.) (1991) *Effective Schools for All*, London: Fulton.

Ainscow, M (1993) Teacher education as a strategy for developing inclusive schools, in R. Slee (ed.) *Is There A Desk With My Name On It? The Politics of Integration*, London: Falmer Press.

Ainscow, M. and Muncy, J. (1981) *Special Needs: Action Programme (SNAP)*, Swansea: Drake Education Associates.

Ainscow, M. and Tweddle, D., (1979) *Preventing Classroom Failure: An Objectives Approach*, Chichester: John Wiley.

Akerman T., Cooper, P., Faupel, A., Gillett, D., Kenwood, P., Leadbetter, P., Mason, E., Matthews, C., Mawper, P., Tweddle, D., Williams, H. and Winteringham, D. P. (1984) *DataPac Users' Guide*, Birmingham: University of Birmingham.

Allan, J. (1996) Foucault and special educational needs: a 'box of tools' for analysing children's experiences of mainstreaming, *Disability and Society*, Vol. 11, no. 2, pp. 219–34.

Allan, J. (1999) *Actively seeking inclusion: Pupils with Special Needs in Mainstream Schools*, London: Falmer Press.

Allan, J. (forthcoming) The aesthetics of disability as a productive ideology, in L. Ware (ed.) *Ideology and the Politics of Disability*, New York: Teachers' College Press.

Armstrong F., Armstrong, D. and Barton L. (eds) (2000) *Inclusive Education: Policy Contexts and Comparative Perspectives*, London: Fulton.

Bailey, J. (1998) Medical and psychological models in special needs education, in C. Clark, A. Dyson, and A. Millward (eds) *Theorising Special Education*, London: Routledge.

Barnes, C. (1988) Disability studies: new or not so new directions? in L. Barton, (ed.) *The Politics of Special Educational Needs*, Lewes: Falmer Press.

Barnes, C. (1990) *Cabbage Syndrome: The Social Construction of Dependence*, Lewes: Falmer Press.

Barnes, C. (1991) *Disabled People in Britain and Discrimination: A case for Anti Discrimination Legislation*, London: Hurst and Co. in association with the British Council of Organizations of Disabled People.

Barnes, C. (1992) Qualitative research: valuable or irrelevant, in *Disability and Society*, Vol. 7, no. 2, pp. 115–24.

Barnes, C. (1996a) Foreword, in J. Campbell and M. Oliver (eds) *Disability Politics: Understanding our Past, Changing our Future*, London: Routledge.

Barnes, C. (1996b) Disability and the myth of the independent researcher, *Disability and Society*, Vol. 11, no. 1, pp. 107–10.

Barton, L. (ed.) (1998) *The Politics of Special Educational Needs*, Lewes: Falmer Press.

Barton, L. (ed.) (1996) *Disability and Society: Emerging Issues and Insights*, London: Longman.

Barton, L. and Tomlinson, S. (eds) (1981) *Special Education: Policy, Practices and Social Issues*, London: Harper and Row.

Barton, L. and Tomlinson, S. (1984) *Special Education and Social Interests*, London: Croom Helm.

Beattie, T. (2000) Diploma/MA assignment: concepts and contexts of special educational needs, unpublished coursework, London: University of London Institute of Education.

Bhabha, H. (1994) *The Location of Culture*, London: Routledge.

Biklen, D. (1977) The politics of institutions, in B. Blatt, D. Biklen and R. C. Bogdan (eds) *An Alternative Textbook in Special Education*, Denver: Love Publishing.

Biklen, D. (ed.) (1985) *Achieving the complete school*, New York: Teachers College Press.

Biklen, D. (1992) *Schooling without labels*, Philadelphia: Temple University Press.

Biklen, D. (1993) *Communication Unbound*, New York: Teachers College Press.

Biklen, D. (1998) Foreword: in C. Kliewer, *Schooling children with Down syndrome*, pp. ix-xiii, New York: Teachers College Press.

Biklen, D. and Cardinal (1997) *Contested Words, Contested Science*, New York: Teachers College Press.

Biklen, D. and Duchan, J. F. (1994) 'I am intelligent': the social construction of mental retardation, *Journal for the Association for Persons with Severe Handicaps*, Vol. 19, no. 3, pp. 173–84.

Bines, H. (1986) *Redefining Remedial Education*, London: Croom Helm.

Booth, T. (1981) Demystifying integration, in W. Swann (ed.) *The Practice of Special Education*, Oxford: Blackwell.

Booth, T. (1983) Policies towards the integration of mentally handicapped children in education, *Oxford Review of Education*, Vol. 9, no. 39, pp. 255–68.

Booth, T. (1987) Introduction to the series: Curricula for All, in T. Booth, P. Potts and W. Swann (eds) *Preventing Difficulties in Learning*, Milton Keynes: Open University Press.

Booth, T. (1996) Stories of exclusion: natural and unnatural selection, in E. Blyth and J. Milner (eds), *Exclusion from School: Inter-Professional Issues for Policy and Practice*, London: Routledge.

Booth, T. (1999) Inclusion and exclusion policy in England: who controls the agenda? in F. Armstrong, D. Armstrong and L. Barton (eds) *Inclusive Education: policy, contexts and comparative perspectives*, London: Fulton.

Booth, T. and Ainscow, M. (eds) (1998) *From Them to Us: An International Study of Inclusion in Education*, London: Routledge.

Booth, T. and Coulby, D. (eds) (1987) *Producing and Reducing Disaffection*, Milton Keynes: Open University Press.

Booth, T. and Potts, P. (eds) (1983) *Integrating Special Education*, Oxford: Blackwell.

Booth, T. and Swann, W. (eds) (1987) *Including Pupils with Disabilities*, Milton Keynes: Open University Press.

Booth, T., Potts, P. and Swann, W. (eds) (1987) *Preventing Difficulties in Learning*, Milton Keynes: Open University Press.

Booth, T., Ainscow, M., Black-Hawkins, K., Vaughan, M. and Shaw, L. (1999) *Index for Inclusion: Developing Learning and Participation in Schools*, Bristol: CSIE.

Brantlinger, E. (1997) Using ideology: cases of nonrecognition of the politics of research and practice in special education, *Review of Educational Research*, Vol. 67, no. 4, pp. 425–59.

Brennan, W. (1985) *Curriculum for Special Needs*, Milton Keynes: Open University Press.

Bryan, L. (2000) Diploma/MA assignment: concepts and contexts of special educational needs, unpublished coursework, London: University of London Institute of Education.

Buckton, A. (2000) Diploma/MA assignment: concepts and contexts of special educational needs, unpublished coursework, London: University of London Institute of Education.

Burgess, L. (2000) Diploma/MA assignment: concepts and contexts of special educational needs, unpublished coursework, London: University of London Institute of Education.

Burt, C. (1937) *The Backward Child*, London: University of London Press.

Carr, W. and Kemmis, S. (1982) *Becoming Critical*, Lewes, Falmer Press.

Clark, C., Dyson, A. and Millward, A. (eds) (1998) *Theorising Special Education*, London: Routledge.

Clark, C., Dyson, A., Millward, A. and Skidmore, D. (1997) *New Directions in Special Needs: Innovations in Mainstream Schools*, London: Cassell.

Clough, P. (1988) Bridging the gap between 'mainstream' and 'special': a curriculum problem, *Journal of Curriculum Studies*, Vol. 20, no. 4, pp. 327–38.

Clough, P. (1996) Again, fathers and sons: self, story and the construction of special educational needs, *Disability and Society*, Vol. 11, no. 1, pp. 71–81.

Clough, P. (1998) Differently articulate? Some indices of disturbed/disturbing voices, in P. Clough and L. Barton (eds) *Articulating with Difficulty: Research Voices in Inclusive Education*, London: Sage/Paul Chapman Publishing.

Clough, P. (1999) Crises of schooling and the 'crisis of representation': the story of Rob, *Qualitative Inquiry*, Vol. 5, no. 3, pp. 428–48.

Clough P. and Barton, L. (eds) (1996) *Making Difficulties: research and the construction of Special Educational Need*, London: Paul Chapman Publishing.

Clough P. and Barton L. (eds) (1998) *Articulating with Difficulty: Research Voices in Inclusive Education*, London: Sage/Paul Chapman Publishing.

Corbett, J. and Barton, L. (1992) *A Struggle for Choice: Students with Special Needs in Transition to Adulthood*, London: Routledge.

Corbett, J. (1996) *Bad-Mouthing: The Language of Special Needs*, London: Falmer Press.

Corbett, J. (1998) *Special Educational Needs in the Twentieth Century: A Cultural Analysis*, London: Cassell.

Corker, M. (1998) *Deaf and Disabled, or Deafness Disabled?* Buckingham: Open University Press.

Corker, M. and French, S. (eds) (1999) *Disability Discourse*, Buckingham: Open University Press.

Creese, A., Daniels, H. and Norwich, B. (1997) *Teacher Support Teams in Primary and Secondary Schools*, London: Fulton.

Daniels, H. (1989) Visual displays as tacit relays of the structure of pedagogic practice, *British Journal of Sociology of Education*, Vol. 10, no. 2, pp. 123–40.

Daniels, H. (ed.) (1993) *Charting the Agenda: Educational Activity after Vygotsky*, London: Routledge.

Daniels, H. (1995) Pedagogic practices, tacit knowledge and discursive discrimination: Bernstein and post-Vygotskian research, *British Journal of Sociology of Education*, Vol. 16, no. 4, pp. 517–32.

Daniels, H. (ed.) (1996a) *An Introduction to Vygotsky*, London: Routledge.

Daniels, H. (1996b) Back to basics: three 'r's for special needs education, *British Journal of Special Education*, Vol. 23, no. 4, pp. 155–62.

Daniels, H. and Anghileri, J. (1995) *Secondary School Mathematics and Special Educational Needs*, London: Cassell.

Daniels, H. and Garner, P. (1999) *Inclusive Education: World Yearbook of Education 1999*, London: Kogan Page.

Daniels, H., Hey, V., Leonard, D. and Smith, M. (1999) Issues of equity in special needs education as seen from the perspective of gender, *British Journal of Special Education*, Vol. 26, no. 4, pp. 189–95.

Daniels, H., Holst, J., Lunt, I. and Johansen, L. (1996) An intercultural comparative study of the relation between different models of pedagogic practice and constructs of deviance, *Oxford Review of Education*, special issue on Vygotsky in education, Vol. 22, no. 1, pp. 63–77.

Daniels, H., Visser, J. and Cole, T. (1999) *Emotional and Behavioural Difficulty in Mainstream Schools*, London: DfEE.

Department of Education and Science (DES) (1978) *Report of the Commission on Special Education* (Warnock Report), London: HMSO.

Derrida, J. (1972) Plato's pharmacy, in *Dissemination* (trans. B. Johnson), Chicago: University of Chicago Press.

Derrida, J. (1998) Spectres of Marx, in Wolfreys, J. (ed.) *The Derrida Reader*: Edinburgh: Edinburgh University Press.

Dessent, T. (1983) Who is responsible for children with special needs? in T. Booth and P. Potts (eds) *Integrating Special Education*, Oxford: Blackwell.

Dessent, T. (1987) *Making the Ordinary School Special*, London: Falmer Press.

Dyson, A. (1981) It's not what you do – it's the way that you do it: setting up a curriculum for less-able high school pupils, *Remedial Education*, Vol. 16, no. 3, pp. 120–3.

Dyson, A. (1985) A curriculum for the 'Educated Man'? *British Journal of Special Education*, Vol. 12, no. 4, pp. 138–9.

Dyson, A. (1990a) Effective learning consultancy: a future role for special needs co-ordinators? *Support for Learning*, Vol. 5, no. 3, pp. 116–27.

Dyson, A. (1990b) Special educational needs and the concept of change, *Oxford Review of Education*. Vol. 16, no. 1, pp. 55–66.

Dyson, A. (1997) Social and educational disadvantage: reconnecting special needs education, *British Journal of Special Education*, Vol. 24, no. 4, 152–7.

Dyson, A. (2000) Personal communication with Peter Clough.

Education Department of Victoria (1984) *Integration in Victorian Education*, Melbourne: Victorian Government Printer.

Evans, J., Dyson, A. and Wedell, K. (1999) *Collaboration for Effectiveness: Empowering Schools to be Inclusive*, Buckingham: Open University Press.

Fasan. A. (2000) Diploma/MA assignment: concepts and contexts of special educational needs, unpublished coursework, London: University of London Institute of Education.

Finkelstein, V. (1980) *Attitudes and Disabled People*, New York: World Rehabilitation Fund.

Fish J. (1985a) Educational Opportunities For All? (The Fish Report) *The Report of the Committee of the Inner London Education Authority on Provision for Special Educational Needs*, London: ILEA.

Fish, J (1985b) Community, co-operation, co-partnership, in *Proceedings of the International Congress of Special Education*, Nottingham, UK.

Florian, L. (1998) An examination of the practical problems associated with the implementation of inclusive education policies, *Support for Learning*, Vol. 13, no. 3, pp. 105–8.

Florian, L. and Pullin, D. (2000) Defining difference: a comparative perspective on legal and policy issues in education reform and special educational needs, in M. Rouse and M. McLaughlin (eds) *Special Education and School Reform in the United States and Britain*, London: Routledge.

Foucault, M. (1977) Intellectuals and power: a conversation between Michel Foucault and Giles Deleuze, in D. Bouchard (ed.) *Language, Counter-Memory, Practice: Selected Essays and Interviews by Michel Foucault*, Oxford: Blackwell.

Freire, P. (1972) *Pedagogy of the Oppressed* (M. B. Ramos, trans.) Harmondsworth: Penguin Books.

French, S. (1992) Memories of school: 1958–1962, in S. O'Keefe (ed.), *Living Proof*, London: Royal National Institute for the Blind.

French, S. (1993) 'Can you see the rainbow?': the roots of denial, in J. Swain, V. Finkelstein, S. French and M. Oliver (eds) *Disabling Barriers – Enabling Environments*, London: Sage.

French, S. (1994) Equal opportunities ... yes please, in L. Keith (ed.) *Mustn't Grumble: Writing by Disabled Women*, London: The Women's Press.

French, S. (1998) Surviving the institution: Working as a visually disabled lecturer in higher education, in D. Malina and S. Maslin-Prothero (eds) *Surviving the Academy: Feminist Perspectives*, London: Falmer Press.

Fulcher, G. (1989) *Disabling Policies? A Comparative Approach to Education Policy and Disability*, London: Falmer Press.

Fulcher, G. (1993) Schools and contests: a reframing of the effective schools debate? in R. Slee (ed.) *Is There a Desk with my Name on It? The Politics of Integration*, Falmer Press: London.

Fulcher, G. (1998) A novel's view of the corporate fantasy, *Campus Review*, 6 May.

Galletley, I. (1976) How to do away with yourself, *Remedial Education*, Vol. 11, no. 3, pp. 149–152.

Giddens, A. (1997) *Sociology*, Cambridge: Polity Press.

Golby, M., and Gulliver, R. J. (1979) Whose remedies, whose ills? A critical review of remedial education, *Remedial Education*, Vol. 11, no. 2, pp. 137–47.

Golby, M. and Gulliver, J. (1985) Whose remedies, whose ills? *Journal of Curriculum Studies*, Vol. 11, no. 2, pp. 137–47.

Hall, R. (2000) Diploma/MA assignment: concepts and contexts of special educational needs, unpublished coursework, London: University of London Institute of Education.

Hasek, J. (1973) *The Good Soldier Sjveik*, Harmondsworth: Penguin.

Her Majesty's Inspectorate (HMI) (1978) *Behaviour Units*, London: HMSO.

Herbert, E. (1998) Included from the start? Managing Early Years settings for all, in P. Clough (ed.) *Managing Inclusive Education: From Policy to Experience*, London: Sage/Paul Chapman Publishing.

Hindess, B. (1986) Actors and social relations, in M. L. Wardell, and S. P. Turner, (eds) *Sociological Theory in Transition*, Winchester, MA: Allen and Unwin.

Hopkins, D., West, M. and Ainscow, M. (1996) *Improving the Quality of Education for All*, London: Fulton.

Kohl, H. (1973) *Reading, How To*, Harmondsworth: Penguin.

Kundera, M. (1986) *The Art of the Novel*, London: Faber and Faber.

Kundera, M. (1991) *Immortality*, London: Faber and Faber.

Lingard, B. (1998) The Disadvantaged Schools Programme: caught between literacy and local management of schools, in *International Journal of Inclusive Education*, no. 2, no. 1, pp. 1–14.

Lipsky, D. K. and Gartner, A. (1997) *Inclusion and School Reform: Transforming America's Classrooms*, Baltimore, MA: Brookes Publishing.

Lunt, I. and Norwich, B. (1999) *Can Effective Schools be Inclusive Schools?* London: Perspectives on Education Policy Series, Institute of Education.

MacGilchrist, B. Myers, K. and Reed, J. (1997) *The Intelligent School*, London: Paul Chapman Publishing.

Mansaray, A. (2000) Diploma/MA assignment: concepts and contexts of special educational needs, unpublished coursework, London: University of London Institute of Education

McBrien, J. (1981) Introducing the EDY Project, *Special Education: Forward Trends*,

Vol. 8, no. 2, pp. 29–30.

McNiff, J. (1988) *Action Research: Principles and Practice*, London: Macmillan.

Mills, C. W. (1970) *The Sociological Imagination*, Harmondsworth: Penquin.

Mittler, P. (1973) Purposes and principles of assessment, in P. Mittler (ed.) *Assessment for Learning in the Mentally Handicapped*, London: Longman.

Mittler, P. (1981) Teacher training for the 21st century, *Special Education: Forward Trends* Vol. 8, no. 2, pp. 8–11.

Mittler, P. (1995) Special needs education: an international perspective, *British Journal of Special Education*, Vol. 22, no. 3, pp. 105–8.

Mittler, P. (1996) Advocates and advocacy, in P. Mittler with V. Sinason, *Changing Policy and Practice for People with Learning Disabilities*, London: Cassell.

Mizon, A. (2000) Diploma/MA assignment: concepts and contexts of special educational needs, unpublished coursework, London: University of London Institute of Education.

Napolitano, S. (1998) My place, in D. McLean, *Beyond barriers: a consultation paper on arts and disability policy*, Web site: http://ndaf.org.Pages/BEYONDBARRIERS

North London School of Physiotherapy for the Visually Handicapped (1981) Promotional Literature, London: NLSPVH.

Norwich, B. (1990) *Reappraising Special Needs Education*, London: Cassell.

Norwich, B. (1993a) Has special educational needs outlived its usefulness? in J. Visser and G. Upton (eds) *Special Education in Britain after Warnock*, London: Fulton.

Norwich, B. (1993b) Ideological dilemmas in special needs education: practitioners' views, *Oxford Review of Education*, Vol. 19, no. 4, pp. 527–46.

Oakley, A. (2000) *Experiments in Knowing: Gender and Method in the Social Sciences*, Cambridge: Polity Press.

Oliver, M. (1983) *Social Work with Disabled People*, London: British Association of Social Workers.

Oliver, M. (1988) The social and political context of educational policy: the case of special needs, in L. Barton (ed.) *The Politics of Special Educational Needs*, London: Falmer Press.

Oliver, M. (1990) *The Politics of Disablement*, Basingstoke: Macmillan.

Oliver, M. (1992) Changing the social relations of research production? *Disability, Handicap and Society*, Vol. 7, no. 2, pp. 101–14.

Parrilla, A. and Daniels, H. (eds) (1998): *Cómo crear y desarrollar un grupo de apoyo entre profesores (How to Set Up and Develop a Teacher Support Team)* Bilbao: Ediciones Mensajero.

Potts, P. (1987) Did they all get into the ark? Blackshaw Nursery, in T. Booth, P. Potts and W. Swann (eds) *Preventing Difficulties in Learning*, Oxford: Blackwell and Open University Press.

Potts, P. (1997) Gender and membership of the mainstream, *International Journal of Inclusive Education*, Vol. 1, no. 2, pp. 175–87.

Potts, P. (1999) Human rights and inclusive education in China: a western perspective, in F. Armstrong and L. Barton (eds) *Disability, Human Rights and Education: Cross-Cultural Perspectives*, Buckingham, Open University Press.

Pratt, W. (2000) Coursework assignment: inclusive education, unpublished coursework, Chatham: Mid-Kent College.

Purdie, S. (2000) Diploma/MA assignment: concepts and contexts of special educational needs, unpublished coursework, London: University of London Institute of Education.

Reason, R., Farrell, P. and Mittler, P. (1990) Changes in assessment, in N. Entwistle (gen. ed.) *Handbook of Educational Ideas and Practices*, pp. 1023–34, London: Routledge.

178     *Theories of Inclusive Education*

Riddell, S. and Brown, S. (eds) (1996) *Special Educational Needs Policy in the 1990s: Warnock in the Market Place*, London: Routledge.

Riddell, S., Adler, M., Farmakopoulou, N. and Mordaunt, E. (forthcoming) Special educational needs and competing policy frameworks in England and Scotland, *Journal of Education Policy*.

Riddell, S., Baron, S. and Wilson, A. (1999) Social capital and people with learning difficulties, *Studies in the Education of Adults*, Vol. 31, no. 1, pp. 49–66.

Riddell, S., Baron, S. and Wilson, A. (forthcoming) The meaning of the learning society for women and men with learning difficulties, *Gender and Education*.

Riddell, S., Baron, S., Stalker, K. and Wilkinson, H. (1997) The concept of the learning society for adults with learning difficulties: human and social capital perspectives, *Journal of Education Policy*, Vol. 12, no. 6, pp. 473–85.

Riddell, S., Brown, S. and Duffield, J. (1994) Parental power and special educational needs: the case of specific learning difficulties, *British Educational Research Journal*, Vol. 20, no. 3, pp. 327–44.

Riddell, S., Dyer, S. and Thomson, G. (1990) Parents, professionals and social welfare models: the implementation of the Education (Scotland) Act 1981, *European Journal of Special Needs, Education*, Vol. 5, no. 2, pp. 96–110.

Riddell, S., Wilson, A. and Baron, S. (1999) Captured customers: people with learning difficulties in the social market, *British Educational Research Journal*, Vol. 25, no. 4, pp. 445–61.

Rouse, M. and Florian, L. (1997) Inclusive education in the marketplace, *International Journal of Inclusive Education*, Vol. 1, no. 4, pp. 323–36.

Santi, L. (2000) Diploma/MA assignment: concepts and contexts of special educational needs, unpublished coursework, London: University of London Institute of Education.

Sayer, J. (1987) *Secondary Schools for All? Strategies for Special Needs*, London: Cassell.

Schonell, F. (1942) *Backwardness in the Basic Subjects*, London: Oliver and Boyd.

Shapiro, J. (1993) *No pity: People with Disabilities Forging a New Civil Rights Movement*, New York: Times Books.

Shumway, D. (1989) *Michel Foucault*, Charlottesville, VA: University Press of Virginia.

Skrtic, T. M. (1991) *Behind Special Education: A Critical Analysis of Professional Culture and School Organisation*, Denver: Love Publishing.

Slee, R. (ed.) (1993) *Is There a Desk with my Name on It? The Politics of Integration*, London: Falmer Press.

Slee, R. (1999) Special education and human rights in Australia: how do we know about disablement, and what does it mean for educators? in F. Armstrong and L. Barton (eds) *Disability, Human Rights and Education: Cross-cultural Perspectives*, Milton Keynes: Open University Press.

Sloterdijk, P. (1987) *Critique of Cynical Reason*, Minneapolis, MN: University of Minnesota Press.

Smith, R. (2000) Gender and Special Education: what makes boys so 'special'? PhD thesis, London: University of London Goldsmiths College.

Sparkes, J. (1999) *Schools, Education and Social Exclusion Case Paper 29*, London: Centre for Analysis of Social Exclusion.

Spiers, S. (2000) Diploma/MA assignment: concepts and contexts of special educational needs, unpublished coursework, London: University of London Institute of Education.

Stenhouse, L. (1975) *An Introduction to Curriculum Research and Development*, London: Heinemann.

Tomlinson, S. (1982) *A Sociology of Special Education*, London: Routledge and Kegan Paul.

Tomlinson, S. (1999) Exclusion: the middle classes and the common good, in H. Daniels and P. Garner (eds) *Inclusive Education: World Yearbook of Education 1999*, London: Kogan Page.

UNESCO (1995) *UNESCO Statistical Yearbook*, Paris: UNESCO.

UPIAS (1976) *The Fundamental Principles of Disability*, London: UPIAS.

Wade, C. M. (1987) I am not one of them, in L. Davis (ed.) *The Disability Studies Reader*, London: Routledge.

Warnock, M. (1999) in Times Education Supplement, 31 December.

Wedell, K. (ed.) (1975) *Orientations in Special Education*, London: John Wiley.

Wedell, K. (1993) Special needs education: the next 25 years, in *Briefings for the National Commission on Education*, London: Heinemann.

Wedell, K. (1995) Making inclusive education ordinary, *British Journal of Special Education*, Vol. 22, no. 3, pp. 100–4.

Wedell, K. (1970) Diagnosing learning difficulty: a sequential strategy, *Journal of Learning Disabilities*, Vol. 3, no. 6, pp. 23–9.

Widlake, P. (1984) Beyond the Sabre-Toothed Curriculum, *Remedial Education*, Vol 19, no. 1, pp. 190–201.

Williams, G. (2000) Coursework assignment: inclusive education, unpublished coursework, Chatham: Mid-Kent College.

Williams, P. (1990) Special educational needs, in N. Entwistle (ed.) *Handbook of Educational Ideas and Practice*, pp. 1020–2, London: Routledge.

Williams, P. (1985) Series Editor's introduction, in W. Brennan *Curriculum for Special Need*, Milton Keynes: Open University Press.

Wolfendale, S. (1993) *Assessing Special Educational Needs*, London: Cassell.

Wolfendale, S. (2000) *Special Needs in the Early Years: Snapshots of Practice*, London: Routledge.

Wolfendale, S. (1987) The evaluation and revision of the 'All About Me' pre-school parent-completed scales, *Early Child Development and Care*, Vol. 1, no. 29 pp. 473–558

Ysseldyke, J. E. (1987) Do tests help in teaching? *Journal of the Association of Child Psychology and Psychiatry*, Vol. 28, no. 1, pp. 21–5.

Zizek, S (1994) The spectre of ideology, in S. Zizek (ed.) *Mapping Ideology*, London:

# Index